Hellenic Studies 43

MULTITEXTUALITY IN
THE HOMERIC *ILIAD*

Recent Titles in the
Hellenic Studies Series

MULTITEXTUALITY IN
THE HOMERIC *ILIAD*

The Witness of the Ptolemaic Papyri

Graeme D. Bird

CENTER FOR HELLENIC STUDIES
Trustees for Harvard University
Washington, DC
Distributed by Harvard University Press
Cambridge, Massachusetts, and London, England
2010

Multitextuality in the Homeric *Iliad*: The Witness of the Ptolemaic Papyri
  By Graeme D. Bird
Copyright © 2010 Center for Hellenic Studies, Trustees for Harvard University
All Rights Reserved.
Published by Center for Hellenic Studies, Trustees for Harvard University, Washington, D.C.
Distributed by Harvard University Press, Cambridge, Massachusetts and London, England

The cover image shows some of the more than 40 fragments of the papyrus P. Tebt. 0899 (papyrus 270 in this book), dated to the middle of the 2nd century BCE. Courtesy of the Center for the Tebtunis Papyri, University of California, Berkeley; thanks to Todd M. Hickey, Assistant Research Papyrologist.

LIBRARY OF CONGRESS CATALOGING-IN-PUBLICATION DATA
Bird, Graeme D.
    Multitextuality in the Homeric Iliad : the witness of the ptolemaic papyri /
  by Graeme D. Bird.
      p.   cm. — (Hellenic studies ; 43)
    In English and ancient Greek.
    Includes bibliographical references and index.
    ISBN 978-0-674-05323-6 (alk. paper)
  1. Homer. Iliad—Criticism, Textual. 2. Homer—Manuscripts. 3. Epic poetry, Greek—
    Criticism, Textual.   I. Title. II. Series.

PA4037.B515 2010
883'.01—dc22   2010023640

Contents

Introduction

IN THIS BOOK I seek to tie together the Parry-Lord theory of oral composition with the evidence of the Ptolemaic papyri of the Homeric *Iliad*. This necessarily includes an examination of the traditional practice of textual criticism, in an effort to show that the text of Homer must be treated rather differently from the texts of classical and biblical authors in general.

Accordingly my first chapter looks both at the principles of textual criticism, and at some of the ways in which they have been applied. The discipline partakes of the elements both of a science and of an art, and some of its most noteworthy practitioners have often had personal characteristics seemingly as "eccentric" as any of the textual evidence I will be considering.

My second chapter moves from classical texts in general to Homer in particular; I seek to show that the Homeric textual evidence is different in nature, not just in degree, from that of other ancient authors. I also note how many scholars, apparently unwilling to acknowledge this difference, have frequently insisted on treating the Homeric evidence in the same way they would any other classical author. I suggest that the nature of the case calls for a different approach: one in which the goal is not—and cannot be—to establish the one true "original" text, since such a thing never existed in the way that it did for authors such as Pindar or Virgil.

In my third chapter I introduce the Ptolemaic papyri of the *Iliad*, first describing their discovery and the initial reactions of scholars, then placing their evidence into the context of other textual evidence of the *Iliad*. I spend some time examining their perhaps most "eccentric" feature—the so-called "plus verses"—including some visual aids in the form of charts and tables that are designed to help the reader grasp a sense of the unusual nature of the evidence. One of my goals is to show that the evidence of the Ptolemaic papyri, small in scale though it may be, should be seen as representative of what must have been a much larger reality; if we had Ptolemaic papyri covering the whole of the *Iliad* (rather than the few passages we do have), we should expect that the proportion of plus (and minus) verses—as well as other significant variation—would have been just as high for the whole as it is for our small but tantalizing sample.

I end Chapter Three with short analyses of some passages from the Ptolemaic papyri—passages which include both plus verses and significant variation within neighboring lines. Although I do not account for all such cases of textual variation, I do seek to show that in these cases (and in others that I might have included) the nature of the variation is "organic"—lines have not been "dropped" into place arbitrarily; rather, they give the appearance of having "grown" in their current locations, in the process modifying their surroundings and resulting in a coherent "version" of an episode that is no less "Homeric"; they may indeed (witness the passages analyzed) be more emotionally intense than the versions with which we are more familiar.

I end with an appendix that contains a list (by no means comprehensive) of some of the terms—particularly Latin—used in traditional textual criticism. Some of these will no doubt be familiar to most classicists, but a few may not. Also in the Appendix are some further examples of cases where the transmission of a "text"—whether written or mathematical or even musical—shares in the same kind of "multitextuality" that I am claiming is exemplified by the Ptolemaic papyri.

I note here that this book will also be available in electronic format, with additional supplementary material, on the Center for Hellenic Studies Web site, URL http://chs.harvard.edu/publications. This will enable further electronic dialogue on the topics discussed in the book, and I welcome opportunities for such conversations.

I have benefited and learned a lot from the prior work of several scholars, including particularly, with respect to the Ptolemaic papyri, that of T. W. Allen, B. M. Bolling, D. F. Sutton, M. J. Apthorp, S. West, and M. L. West. The fact that my own conclusions may not always concur with theirs does not lessen my appreciation for their diligent and careful scholarship. I offer my grateful thanks to Carolyn Higbie, Timothy Boyd, and Albert Henrichs for helpful comments and advice on earlier versions of this project. I express my deep appreciation to Leonard Muellner for his regular and friendly encourage-ment, and to Gregory Nagy for his constant support and for being a model of clarity of thought and expression. Finally, my sincere thanks to Jill Curry Robbins for her editorial wisdom, good humor, and patience.

MULTITEXTUALITY IN
THE HOMERIC *ILIAD*

Chapter 1

Textual Criticism as Applied to Classical and Biblical Texts

THE PRIMARY GOAL OF TEXTUAL CRITICISM has traditionally been to establish the actual text that the author wrote, so far as this is possible.[1] This needs to be done because, in the case of Classical and biblical authors (and sometimes in the case of more recent texts), the autograph, or author's original manuscript, no longer exists. In its place there are surviving manuscripts, each of which is a copy of an earlier manuscript, often at an unknown number of steps removed from the autograph.

The situation just described includes three assumptions: first, that there actually was an author; second, that the author left behind an original manuscript; and third, that this original is worth trying to reconstruct. The further complication frequently arises in which it appears that the author has left more than one manuscript of a particular work, leaving the question as to which of these versions should be treated as the authoritative one (with the default generally, but not always, being the last one). I mention this because recently there has been vigorous debate over the second and third of these three assumptions, especially in relation to texts dating from the time of Shakespeare on, but also in connection with biblical and classical texts. However, for the sake of the present discussion I will proceed with these three assumptions in mind.

The texts of classical and biblical authors have come down to us in widely varying states of abundance: at one extreme, for example, the two chief works of the Roman historian Tacitus (*Annales* and *Historiae*) each survive in a single medieval manuscript[2]; at the other, Homer's *Iliad* is currently represented by more than 1,900 manuscripts (at least 1,500 of which are on papyrus, although many of these of a fragmentary nature).[3] And for the Greek New Testament,

---

[1] See Maas 1958:1; Renehan 1969:2; West 1973:8.

[2] Reynolds 1983:406–407.

[3] West 2001:88–129 lists more than 700 published papyri plus a further 850 or so that are thus far unpublished; in addition he includes about 140 papyri containing Homeric glossaries,

there survive more than 3,000 Greek manuscripts (interestingly, with papyrus comprising a tiny minority—94, or around 3 percent). This last figure does not include more than 2,000 "lectionaries" (containing portions of the Gospels and Epistles arranged for daily and weekly lessons), "versions" (translations into languages such as Latin, Syriac, Coptic, Gothic, Georgian, and Armenian), or quotations in early church fathers; each of these different sources of evidence plays a significant role in efforts to establish the original text of the Greek New Testament.[4]

How one approaches the process of creating an edition of a Classical author will obviously be affected by the quantity of extant evidence. The overall procedure will also be determined by the textual editor's *modus operandi* (on which more below), but generally follows the same set of steps, traditionally given by their Latin names[5]:

i)   *recensio*: sorting through and collating the surviving manuscript evidence.

ii) *examinatio*: an attempt to establish the earliest possible version of the text.

iii) *emendatio*: correcting the text when none of the surviving manuscripts appears to preserve the correct reading; this may include making a conjecture (see below). Also referred to by the term *divinatio*, a term which imparts perhaps a little too much mystique to the process.[6]

The seemingly straightforward elements of textual criticism are: whenever the surviving manuscripts agree on a piece of text, this most likely represents the original; whenever they disagree over a particular passage, be it something as apparently trivial as the alternate spelling of a word or the use of a different word, or something as significant as the omission of a whole section in one manuscript and its inclusion in another, one must decide which of the two or perhaps more options is the best—in other words, which version represents the original words of the author?

---

commentaries, and *scholia minora*; also nearly 50 others containing quotations of lines from the *Iliad*. West further uses nineteen medieval minuscule manuscripts, some of which contain complete texts of the *Iliad*. T. W. Allen had listed a total of about 190 medieval manuscripts, and in his *editio maior* of 1931 he attempts to cite each for every variant reading, leading to a critical apparatus often taking up more space than the text itself.

4   Aland 1987:72–184; Metzger 1992:36–94; Epp and Fee 1993:4–6.

5   For a helpful account, which is written to describe the textual criticism of Latin texts but applies equally well to Greek, see Tarrant 1995:106f. See also Reynolds and Wilson 1991:207ff.

6   See below, n83.

The difficulties arise when one actually looks closely at this process of deciding. What may at first glance seem like a simple matter of preferring one reading over another—and occasionally it may be that simple—in reality is determined both by the nature of the evidence and by the proclivity—some might even say the eccentricity—of the textual editor. Indeed, as we shall see, sometimes in spite of the fact that all extant witnesses present the same text, nevertheless it is clear (at least to some) that the text is "corrupt" and needs to be "emended."

A major part of the initial process of *recensio* is the grouping into families of the extant manuscripts, an analysis also known as stemmatics, in order to discover how errors that arose early in the textual tradition have been passed down with repeated copying. In other words, manuscripts which contain such "shared errors" are most likely members of a "family," and have passed on their errors from one "generation" of copying to the next, much as members of a human family pass on their various genes to their offspring. By so doing one is able to decide which manuscripts are "dependent" upon others, and hence are of less importance in determining the correct text. Such dependent manuscripts are known as *codices descripti*, and the process whereby they are "removed" from further consideration is called *eliminatio codicum descriptorum*.[7] The New Testament scholar J. A. Bengel (1687–1752) was among the first to stress that manuscripts must be *weighed*, not merely *counted*[8]; in other words, if one or more manuscripts can be shown to depend on (i.e. derive from) an older manuscript—which is extant—then these dependent later manuscripts contribute little or nothing in terms of weight to any debate over variant readings.[9] Thus the evidence for and against a particular reading will always take into account this factor of dependence, rather than any simple counting of numbers of manuscripts.[10]

---

[7] For these and other Latin terms, see Appendix B.

[8] Bengel 1742, Admonition 12 in his preface.

[9] However, Reeve (1987:1ff.) argues, firstly, that it is impossible to prove that any particular manuscript is "exclusively derived" from another, and secondly, that so-called *codices descripti*, far from being *inutiles*, can be useful both for textual editors and also for shedding light on the history of the transmission of the text. See esp. p. 8.

[10] An example of the avoidance of this principle involves the debate over the merits of the "King James Version" of the Bible. KJV proponents argue that the overwhelming preponderance in *numbers* of manuscripts supporting the "Textus Receptus" proves its superiority, whereas the majority of scholars point to a) the widespread dependence of these (late) manuscripts upon only a few exemplars, and b) the significant number of much earlier manuscripts whose text shows much less evidence of either contamination or the "smoothing out" of difficult passages. For a critique of the so-called "Majority Text" and of the arguments used to support it, see Epp and Fee 1993:183–208. For a modern and more nuanced defense, see Robinson 2002.

I note at this point that the history of textual criticism, particularly over the last three centuries, has involved a significant mutual influence between the fields of classical and biblical literature. I refer in particular to such scholars as Richard Bentley, who achieved breakthroughs in both Homeric and New Testament (NT) studies[11]; J. G. Eichhorn, the Old Testament scholar who had an important influence upon F. A. Wolf and his *Prolegomena*[12]; and Karl Lachmann, who refined to an unprecedented degree the method of the study of manuscripts, as exemplified in his editions of Lucretius and the Greek New Testament.[13] In addition, the quantity of surviving material available for studying the text of Homer is far greater than for any other classical author, and is only exceeded in ancient Greek literature by the abundance of textual evidence pertaining to the New Testament.[14] It is reasonable to expect that techniques which have been developed to deal with such a wealth of variant readings in this latter text will in all likelihood be of assistance in handling the smaller—but equally, if not more divergent—quantity of variants that survive in our witnesses to the text of Homer. I shall therefore refer at times to text-critical methods employed by scholars working in this closely related field.

Bengel is also considered the first to formulate the canon of textual criticism which regards the more difficult reading as preferable to the less difficult—the primacy of the *lectio difficilior*, or in his words *proclivi scriptioni praestat ardua*[15] (also *lectio difficilior potior/melior*). The scribe, in his role as copyist, is most unlikely to change a word or passage which reads satisfactorily into something which presents problems of clarity, smoothness, or unusual grammar. He is much more likely to "smooth out" passages which already present such "difficulties": this smoothing out process may be conscious or even unconscious. Thus if we are confronted with two variant readings in a particular passage, one "easier" and the other "harder," we need to be able to explain how the two arose. A common scenario is that the harder reading is original (i.e. *lectio difficilior potior*), with the easier one having been corrupted from it by the scribe's attempts to facilitate a difficult construction, or perhaps in order to harmonize the passage with another which conflicts with it in some way. In NT textual criticism harmonization is especially relevant in two cases. Firstly, when an account in one Gospel does not agree exactly with

---

[11] See Pfeiffer 1976:156f.
[12] See Wolf 1985. Wolf's translators discuss his debt to Eichhorn on pp. 18–26; and Wolf himself frequently makes comparisons between Homeric and Old Testament textual study, e.g. pp. 49–52.
[13] Pfeiffer 1976:90.
[14] See above, pp. 1–2.
[15] See Metzger 1992:112.

that in another, there is often a variant reading that aligns one account with the other. Secondly, when a NT writer quotes from the Hebrew Bible (usually via the Septuagint or LXX, the third-century BCE Greek translation used by Hellenistic Jews, and apparently also by most NT writers), and the quotation does not exactly match the original, there is frequently a variant that brings the quotation into line with the original.

An example of the harmonization of differing Gospel accounts involves the Lord's Prayer, which occurs in two Gospels, Matthew and Luke. The version more familiar to most readers is the former, which starts:

πάτερ ἡμῶν, ὁ ἐν τοῖς οὐρανοῖς, ἁγιασθήτω τὸ ὄνομά σου. . .

Our Father, the one in the heavens, let your name be hallowed . . .

Matthew 6:9

When we come to Luke's account, the "best" (needless to say, this term begs the question) and oldest manuscripts give a shorter version:

πάτερ, ἁγιασθήτω τὸ ὄνομά σου. . .

Father, let your name be hallowed . . .

Luke 11:2

It is generally believed (for reasons not gone into here) that the Matthean version is older, and hence "original." Not surprisingly, several manuscripts, some early, give the longer reading for Luke, illustrating one or more ancient scribes' efforts to bring Luke's account into harmony with Matthew's. In fact the urge to harmonize in this case would have been fairly compelling; of the majority of manuscripts which did not thus succumb, the NT textual scholar Bruce Metzger comments, "it is remarkable that such a variety of early witnesses managed to resist what must have been an extremely strong temptation to assimilate the Lukan text to the much more familiar Matthean form."[16] Presumably reverence for the text will have played an important role in this.

For an instance of assimilation to the Septuagint, I refer to the anonymous letter to the Hebrews, chapter 1, verses 11–12. These verses are part of a quotation from Psalm 102, verse 26. The Septuagint (in which the passage is numbered Psalm 101, verse 27, following the Hebrew Bible, in which the title of the psalm frequently counts as the first verse) reads as follows:

καὶ πάντες ὡς ἱμάτιον παλαιωθήσονται,

---

[16] Metzger 1971:154.

καὶ ὡσεὶ περιβόλαιον ἀλλάξεις (v.l. ἑλίξεις) αὐτούς,
καὶ ἀλλαγήσονται.

And they will all wear out like a cloak,
And like a garment you will exchange them (v.l. roll them up),
And they will be exchanged.

In the "best" and oldest manuscripts of the NT Hebrews passage, the words ὡς ἱμάτιον are inserted a second time into the quotation as follows:

καὶ πάντες ὡς ἱμάτιον παλαιωθήσονται,
καὶ ὡσεὶ περιβόλαιον ἑλίξεις (v.l. ἀλλάξεις) αὐτούς,
<u>ὡς ἱμάτιον</u> καὶ ἀλλαγήσονται.

And they will all wear out like a cloak,
And like a garment you will roll (v.l. exchange) them up,
And <u>like a cloak</u> they will be exchanged.

However, most manuscripts omit these words in an apparent attempt to harmonize the NT text to that of the LXX. Metzger remarks that the author of Hebrews inserted the words "to show that the metaphor of the garment is continued. The absence of the words from most witnesses is the result of conformation to the text of the Septuagint."[17] (I note also that most NT manuscripts read ἑλίξεις rather than ἀλλάξεις; in two exceptional cases, one the famed ℵ, or "Codex Sinaiticus," the original ἀλλάξεις has been altered by a later scribe to ἑλίξεις.)

Of course, not all textual corruption results from a scribe's conscious (or unconscious) efforts to make his text easier to read. Many examples of variant readings have their origin in simple mis-copying—for whatever reason (simple carelessness, tiredness, bad light, etc.) a scribe drops one or more letters, skips a word or line, writes one letter for another, etc. A. E. Housman[18] gives a useful list of errors involving transposition of letters, under various subheadings (for each example the former reading is that considered correct, the latter a corruption of it):

Trajection of one letter:
cadere in ter**ram** ~ cade**rem** in terra   (Lucretius *De Rerum Natura* II 209)

Inversion of two letters:
amnis ~ **ma**nis   (Virgil *Georgics* I 115)

---

[17] Metzger 1971:663.
[18] Housman 1903:livff.

Inversion of three letters:
> **vo**mere ~ **mo**vere   (Virgil *Georgics* II 203)

Metathesis of syllables:
> mini-**me** ~ **me**-mini   (Plautus *Miles Gloriosus* 356)

Transposition of two letters across an intervening space:
> ver**s**arent ~ **s**ervarent   (Propertius IV 1 129)

Rearrangement of four or more letters:
> **et nig**ras ~ **integ**ras   (Propertius III 5 24)

I have given only one example under each heading; Housman includes twenty or thirty or more, as well as copious examples of what he calls "further change," for example:

> visceribus aerari ~ vi caesaris rebus   (Cicero *De domo sua* 23)

This kind of corruption often results in the substitution of a simpler word for a less familiar one, but it also may lead to a text which is actually harder to read, or even completely unintelligible. In such instances, the principle of *lectio difficilior* is not necessarily going to apply.[19]

Sometimes a subsequent scribe may attempt to correct the error, either successfully or otherwise. Housman[20] gives further examples from verse, where meter has been a factor in the attempts of scribes to "repair" a faulty line. Below is a case where haplography (see the Appendix) has caused a word or phrase to drop out, and the demands of meter have led to another word or phrase being inserted into the *lacuna*. First the original text:

> seu stupor huic studio sive est insania nomen
> > omnis ab hac cura <u>cura</u> levata mea est

> But whether "trance" or "madness" be the name for this pursuit,
> > 'twas by such pains that all my pain was lightened.[21]
> > > Ovid *Tristia* I.11.11–12

Evidently the second occurrence of the word "cura" was dropped, and the gap later filled with a metrical (and semantic) equivalent, so that virtually all manuscripts present the reading:

> seu stupor huic studio sive est insania nomen
> > omnis ab hac cura <u>mens re</u>levata mea est

---

[19] See variant b in the passage from Plato's *Timaeus*, below, pp. 19–20.
[20] Housman 1903:lixff.
[21] Translation from Goold 1998.

> . . . all my mind was relieved from this pain

According to Housman, someone thoroughly familiar with Ovid's style would have sensed that "something has gone wrong" just by noticing, as he puts it, the "aimless change from 'huic studio' to 'hac cura.'" However it took the discovery of the correct text in an inscription to compel editors to print a reading that had not survived in any manuscript. Housman expends much energy in chastising those who are too timid to depart from the manuscript tradition when circumstances call for such action: "to do so would involve recognizing that all the mss., not only some of them, are deeply interpolated; and to recognize this would cause them discomfort."[22] A modern editor of Ovid is more willing to accept the discomfort: "a striking error at [Ovid *Tristia*] I. 11. 12 shows that the whole tradition may on occasion be interpolated."[23]

Finally, I give from Housman an example of a line which is presented by the manuscripts, but which is "unscannable":

> an caelum nobis ultro **natura corruptum**
> **deferat** aut aliquid quo non consueuimus uti.
>
> Whether nature of herself brings to us an infected sky
> or something we are not accustomed to experience . . .[24]
>
> Lucretius *De Rerum Natura* VI 1135–1136

The original reading according to Housman (essentially similar translation):

> an caelum nobis **corruptum deferat ultro**
> natura aut aliquid quo non consueuimus uti.

After explaining how these two lines arose by means of various corruptions, Housman concludes by saying, " 'natura corruptum' could be scanned, in the ages of faith, by many a humble Christian; for true religion enabled men not only to defy tortures but to shorten the first syllables . . ." of words such as *corruptum.*[25]

In some cases respect or even reverence for the text may cause the corrupted passage, unintelligible though it is, to be faithfully transmitted down to the present.[26] An example comes from Plutarch's *Moralia* 388c, where the

---

[22] Housman 1903:lx.

[23] Goold 1988:xxxix. He is evidently using the term "interpolated" in a somewhat different sense from how I use it in chaps. 2 and following. Goold continues: "and none of the 60-odd manuscripts available inspires special confidence in its readings or permits us to ignore them."

[24] Translation from Smith 1992.

[25] Ibid. One notes the type of dry humor inspired by encounters with textual corruption.

[26] This is especially common in the Hebrew Bible, where an impossible form is regularly left in

original ὁμιλία (which is actually a modern conjecture, but evidently the original reading) has been corrupted into ὃ μὴ διὰ; though meaningless, the latter reading was nevertheless copied into subsequent manuscripts and in fact helped in the restoration of the original.[27] The process of corruption in this case is easy to see when capitals are used: OMIΛIA → O MH ΔIA. The confusion of H for I involves itacism—an aural confusion,[28] illustrating the fact that ancient and medieval readers, even if alone, would read aloud; alternatively the error could have arisen through the dictation process. The variation between Δ and Λ (and often A) is a very frequent confusion, in this case based on visual similarity (but only for capitals). In addition, since documents were written without word division, instances of mis-segmentation such as this were frequent.[29]

In addition, one must beware of concluding that just because a particular manuscript happens to be full of scribal errors, its underlying text is therefore also of inferior quality. Witness the case of a New Testament papyrus, P46, where the scribe has very carelessly copied an exemplar of high quality: "we must here be careful to distinguish between the very poor work of the scribe who penned it and the basic text which he so poorly rendered . . . once they [the scribe's own errors] have been discarded, there remains a text of outstanding (though not absolute) purity."[30]

This brings us to the question of the quality of manuscripts, that is, the quality of the text to which they bear witness; and this in turn leads us to the spectrum of text-critical methodologies. Textual evidence is generally divided into two categories: *external*, i.e. the details of a manuscript's date, provenance, stemmatic relationships with other manuscripts, etc.; and *internal*, i.e. the nature of the variant reading itself—its grammaticality, stylistic features, etc. The textual critic is always having to weigh these two types of evidence, and, as often as not, either consciously or otherwise, will usually tend to emphasize one more than the other when making decisions about variants. Internal

---

the body of the text, with a footnote presenting the correct form. Because in Hebrew vowels are treated as a sort of "overlay" to the consonants—and are thus not considered sacred, the correct vowels are written in the text in conjunction with the incorrect consonants, generally giving an unpronounceable form.

[27] Another branch of the tradition passed down an intelligible but less helpful variant: ὁμοιότητι—Renehan (1969:48–49) characterizes this as a "conscious conjecture."

[28] See Appendix B. Also Horrocks 1997:67–70 and 102–105, who however does not use the term "itacism."

[29] Renehan 1969:48–49.

[30] Zuntz 1946:212–213. This particular study was in reference to the text of 1 Corinthians and Hebrews. Cited in Epp and Fee 1993:128.

evidence can be further subdivided into a) *transcriptional* and b) *intrinsic* types.[31] The former tends to deal with accidental changes to the text, and involves deciding between variants based on a consideration of how a scribe might have unconsciously altered a reading, due to such things as *homoeoteleuton* (words, phrases, or lines with the same ending; cf. *homoeomeson* and *homoeoarchon*),[32] mistaking of one letter for another, and so forth. Intrinsic evidence is what causes the editor to ask which of the available readings is most likely to be what the author wrote, based on considerations of style, vocabulary, thought patterns, and the like.

When we consider the various ways of approaching textual criticism, we find that there exists a wide range of methodologies. At one end of the spectrum, an editor might decide to follow one manuscript (or family of manuscripts) exclusively, departing from it only in cases of obvious corruption, and otherwise virtually ignoring all other evidence; this is the methodology of the *codex optimus*. To a large degree the earliest editors of classical (and biblical) texts tended to follow one or at most a small number of manuscripts, while ignoring the bulk of the evidence, which often contained better readings. Part of their justification was the fact that access to widely scattered documents was not yet convenient enough to allow full exploitation of all relevant textual evidence; as such access opened up, with improvements in modes of travel, as well as the use of photography, scholars began to use the full range of available documentation. In addition, these earlier textual editors were frequently constrained by the existence of an "entrenched vulgate"—a widely accepted text which they felt compelled to print (especially in the case of the New Testament), while relegating variant readings to the critical apparatus.[33] Although this approach is now far less frequent than in the past, Joseph Bédier (in the field of Old French literature) earlier last century advocated a return to this use of a "best text" which is only corrected in the case of obvious scribal errors, attacking the fundamentally different methodology of stemmatics.[34] One of the reasons for his hostility towards stemmatics was that a disproportionate number of stemmata, as constructed by editors, contain only two branches, a situation which allows the editor undue discretion. For if both branches present different readings, the editor must make the final choice, whereas if there are three or more branches, and two are in agreement against the third, then one is supposed to choose the "majority reading."[35]

---

[31] Epp and Fee 1993:14–15.
[32] See Appendix B.
[33] Reynolds and Wilson 1991:209.
[34] See Speer 1995:394ff.
[35] Tarrant 1995:112f.

Criticism of the *codex optimus* methodology has been severe: Wolf himself condemns scholars and editors who depend excessively and slavishly upon one exemplar, as well as those who use variant readings only when an obvious textual problem appears.[36] Housman, never one to hold back when an opportunity for colorful polemics presented itself, suggested that it would need "divine intervention" to bring it about that "the readings of a MS are right whenever they are possible and impossible whenever they are wrong"; and further that such divine intervention "might have been better employed elsewhere."[37] Tanselle characterizes the "best text" approach as illogical, "a critical approach that embodies a distrust of critical judgment."[38] Reynolds and Wilson point out that the "best manuscript" of an author, if such really exists, can be determined only by methodically going through all the "significant" evidence—i.e. the variants of all seemingly important manuscripts—and by comparing those passages where the evidence diverges, assessing which manuscript gives the "correct" reading more often than any other.[39] My putting such terms as "significant" and "correct" inside quotation marks should alert the reader to the fact that the whole procedure involves critical judgment and experience, and is not to be reduced to some simple formula as the doctrine of the *codex optimus* seems to do: in fact, this latter approach almost boils down to an escape from the complexities of thoroughly examining the evidence and making what are sometimes very difficult decisions.[40]

The other extreme involves the methodology whereby external evidence is virtually ignored, and variants are weighed purely on the basis of their intrinsic (rather than transcriptional, as it appears in practice) internal probability, regardless of the number or quality of the manuscripts supporting such a variant. In NT studies this methodology is sometimes labeled as "rigorous eclecticism"; the chief criticism of this method is that a significant degree of objectivity is lost, and decisions on variants tend to be based on the editor's preference for internal criteria.[41] Approaching textual variants in this way could conceivably lead to the scenario of a reading which is represented solely

---

[36] Wolf 1985:43–45.

[37] Housman 1903:xxxii, quoted in Tarrant 1995:111.

[38] Tanselle 1995:21–22.

[39] Reynolds and Wilson 1991:216–218.

[40] Cf. Tanselle 1995:20, who discusses the "falsity of saying that 'editorial insight is always less reliable than even the most unreliable documents.' "

[41] Epp and Fee 1993:15, where the methods of one of the chief exponents of rigorous eclecticism, G. D. Kilpatrick, are criticized. In Black 2002:101–123, J. K. Elliott titles his chapter "The Case for *Thoroughgoing* Eclecticism" (my emphasis). One notes the suggestive labels given to these various positions.

in one late manuscript being chosen, based on stylistic and other criteria, in preference to one which appears in all other texts, both early and late.

In between these two extremes lies a middle path—what has been called "rational eclecticism" (or "reasoned eclecticism"[42])—where both internal and external evidence play a part:[43] variants are examined and decisions made based on the principle of the *lectio difficilior*; also by following the rule that it should be possible to show how the correct reading has been corrupted into the incorrect; and by counting and weighing manuscript support for each reading—which process naturally includes evaluating each manuscript in terms of its overall textual quality. In practice editors often tend to tilt more to the external or the internal evidence: the celebrated NT textual critic F. J. A. Hort reflects the former tendency when he says "knowledge of documents should precede final judgment upon readings."[44] For the latter emphasis, compare Richard Bentley's famous dictum *nobis et ratio et res ipsa centum codicibus potiores sunt*, 'reason and the facts are worth more to us than a hundred manuscripts'; for him the evidence of the manuscripts had to take second place to factors of sense and style,[45] which is not say that he ignored such evidence; rather for him it could never be the final arbiter in any decision over readings.[46] Compare the more recent statement that in situations where it is not a case of demonstrable error, "most editors do indeed evaluate variants on internal grounds before accepting the results yielded by stemmatic analysis."[47]

In the case of most classical authors, there is not enough evidence to worry excessively about pitting external and internal factors against each other—in fact often it may be obvious that the correct reading has not survived at all, and a conjecture is called for. In many cases, though, one is able to create a stemma which displays the dependence of later manuscripts on earlier ones

---

[42] As in the title of chap. 2 of Black 2002: "The Case for Reasoned Eclecticism" (pp. 77–100) by M. W. Holmes. Grenfell and Hunt 1906:75 (to be discussed further in chap. 3) recommend the use of "judicious eclecticism" in dealing with the unusual texts of the recently discovered Ptolemaic papyri of Homer.

[43] See again Wolf 1985, who talks about the *sense* (internal evidence) and the *authority* (external evidence) of readings.

[44] Westcott and Hort 1882:31; quoted in Epp and Fee 1993:127.

[45] Quoted in Tarrant 1995:96; Tarrant's translation of Bentley.

[46] However, Bentley's excesses in the practice of emendation are well known; for a humorous example of a "logical" but foolish emendation of a line of Horace, see Reynolds and Wilson 1991:186.

[47] Tarrant 1995:107. Also his remark on the same page that "a stemma can describe only what is likely to be true in the majority of cases; it cannot overrule the critic's judgment of any particular instance."

in the form of a family tree. In some cases all surviving manuscripts can thus be successfully traced back to an "archetype," i.e. the document from which all subsequent copies derive. In the optimal situation, this would in fact be what the author himself wrote, in other words, the "autograph"; in less ideal (but more frequent) cases one can get back to an archetype, without being certain as to whether it is also the original author's version. In practice one can never be sure whether one's reconstructed archetype is in fact the same as or even close to the original autograph; indeed often an archetype can be determined, but one which is patently corrupt and in need of emendation.[48] In the process of creating a stemma, one has to take into account such factors as the age of manuscripts (determined by paleographical analysis as well as internal datable references), the geographical location or provenance (and manuscripts, especially papyri, were often copied in one place and transported to another[49]), and the elusive "quality" of the text: bad copies can be made from good exemplars[50]; and while old manuscripts (especially papyri) may often appear to be the most faithful transmitters of the original text because of their age,[51] one should not thereby rule out readings from later manuscripts— pithily epitomized by G. Pasquali in the words *recentiores, non deteriores*, 'later, not inferior.'[52]

While it might appear that an archetype not too far removed in time from the original autograph gives grounds for thinking one has a text very close to the autograph, at least one scholar warns that textual corruptions tend to be the most frequent and even the most severe in the period immediately

---

[48] See n55 below.
[49] See Turner 1968. On pp. 49–51 Turner discusses papyri which were written outside Egypt and brought in subsequently: places of writing include Ravenna, Paphlagonia, and Rome; although the examples he discusses are documentary and not literary papyri, the possibility is always present that literary papyri as well could "travel" some distance from their place of origin.
[50] See n26 above.
[51] For the NT, I note the criticism in Epp and Fee 1993:42–44 and 94–96 of the "excessive" regard for the papyri of the NT held by Aland, as discussed in Aland 1987:56–64 and 83–95. Aland seems to use the age of these papyri (the earliest datable to 125 CE) to justify his view that they hold the key to the original text; Epp and Fee, however, point to the fact that all the papyri come from Egypt, and that it is most unlikely that texts from one location can be confidently accepted as representative of the NT text in general—especially as it is improbable that any of the originals were actually written in Egypt. Compare M. van der Valk's modified version of a statement of Lehrs: "Thou shalt not fall on thy knees before the papyri," in van der Valk 1964:532n6. Van der Valk uses this statement in support of his low view of the early papyri of Homer and other classical Greek authors such as Euripides.
[52] The title of chap. four of Pasquali 1952. Already in 1882 Westcott and Hort (p. 31) had commented on the "occasional preservation of comparatively ancient texts in comparatively modern mss."

following the writing of the autograph.[53] And what is worse, of course, is that, although the archetype was often near chronologically to the autograph, that was "precisely the period of time when, by definition, no cross-checking from other MSS. was done and when the text's transmission was not yet submitted to academic, editorial, or ecclesiastical surveillance."[54] Thus if the archetype itself is corrupt, the only way to correct it is by the process of conjectural emendation.[55] Another scholar writes of the way in which classicists (as well as biblical scholars) can develop almost a reverence for the author's original text, in spite of the fact that we can never know with certainty that we have such a text[56]; correspondingly, one can tend to denigrate manuscripts, seeing them merely as imperfect vehicles transmitting an idealized original.[57]

In the least desirable (but still frequent, perhaps the most frequent) situation, the phenomenon of contamination (Latin *contaminatio*), or "horizontal influence," will have taken place, causing errors to cross stemmatic lines in a way which obscures or even obliterates family relationships. Contamination occurs whenever a scribe does not merely copy his manuscript from an exemplar—this by itself would result in a straightforward "vertical" relationship between the two documents, with most if not all of the exemplar's errors being transmitted to the copy, allowing the copy to be recognized as being "dependent" upon the exemplar—but in addition he "checks" or "collates" his work against a third manuscript, one which often comes from a different part of the "family tree," or stemma. This third manuscript typically has its own distinctive characteristics, i.e. errors, and perhaps good or "original" readings which in other documents have been corrupted; it is thus "independent" of the scribe's exemplar. In this way there arises a horizontal relationship between the second and third manuscripts—i.e. contamination. The foregoing assumes, of course, that the scribe actually does change his text to make it conform with the third manuscript; in some cases scribes do make such corrections, in other cases they leave their new copy as it is; they may even do a combination of the two, i.e. leave their new copy as it is and indicate in the margin that another

---

[53] Koester 1987:41. See also Benedict Einarson, in Renehan 1969:32: "Many of the variants in the text of the New Testament arose before these writings became canonical." See Epp and Fee 1993:127 for criticism of this viewpoint.

[54] Strugnell 1974:552.

[55] Housman 1903:xl: after the work of *recensio* and *examinatio* are done, we have before us "an archetype . . . corrupt and interpolated; and now begins the business of correcting this."

[56] Tarrant 1995:97.

[57] In Denniston and Page 1957:xxxviii, for example, Page writes of the manuscript "cod. G" (of Aeschylus' *Agamemnon*) that its value "could not be less than it is without entirely ceasing to exist."

reading exists, a practice which gives rise to marginal and other notes known as *scholia*.[58]

As an illustration of a simple case of contamination, consider the diagram below (Figure 1), which represents a hypothetical relationship between extant and lost manuscripts: it is a simple example of a *stemma codicum*, or family tree of manuscripts. The uppercase Greek letter Omega (Ω) stands for the presumed archetype, or ancestor of all manuscripts in this particular family; the lower-case Greek letters stand for non-extant manuscripts that are assumed once to have existed (and to have been exemplars for the next "generation," i.e. "hyparchetypes"); and Roman letters stand for manuscripts that are extant.

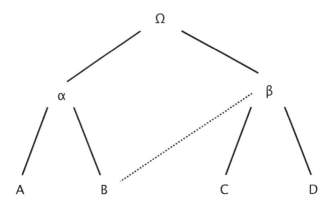

Figure 1. Example of a *stemma codicum*, or family tree of manuscripts.

Without contamination, manuscripts A and B would clearly belong to the same branch, deriving from the lost manuscript α; similarly C and D would derive from β. But suppose the scribe who copied B from α also checked and collated his new manuscript with β, to which he had access (although we do not). This would give rise to characteristics in B that indicate some relation-ship with the right-hand branch, and would thus cloud the picture in terms of clear "vertical" dependency, not to mention make an accurate stemma harder to construct. Such "horizontal" influence is indicated here by the dotted line.

The fact of contamination might not at first seem to be a problem; after all if scribes check their work against other manuscripts surely their final product will be of a higher quality. However, when one is weighing one variant

---

[58] A good example of a manuscript which has been carefully "collated," leading both to "correc-tions" and to the recording of variants in the margins, is the medieval *Iliad* manuscript Venetus A, on which more will be said elsewhere in this book.

reading against another, such a weighing must take into account the weights of the individual manuscripts (as discussed above); independent manuscripts or branches of the stemma carry more weight than those which show some dependence on each other. Thus if a particular reading is shared by two independent branches of the stemma, such as B and C in the diagram above (and thus presumably going back to both α and β, and even to the archetype Ω), it carries more weight than if it appeared in B alone (i.e. α alone, and therefore quite possibly an error that was not in the archetype Ω). But after contamination has occurred, B's weight (regarding the reading in question) now derives, at least in part, and perhaps solely, from β, the exemplar of C, and thus the reading loses a lot of its significance and may even fall out of consideration altogether.[59]

In cases of extreme contamination, precise textual affinity can become so uncertain that the creation of a stemma becomes difficult or even impossible. This is in fact the case with several classical works, such as Virgil's *Aeneid*,[60] as well as the text in general of the Greek New Testament.[61] As we shall see, similar difficulties have plagued those who would create a stemma for the manuscripts of Homer; however I shall argue that in Homer's case both the explanation and the solution are rather different from those applicable to most ancient works.[62]

The previous discussion has been dealing only with external evidence—internal evidence would also play a part in such a weighing of evidence, but the point is that contamination frequently weakens the force of external evidence, by lessening or even eliminating the importance of a manuscript previously thought to be of value. The problems caused by contamination, and the limitations it imposes on the stemmatic method,[63] have not always been fully recognized; Paul Maas' book on textual criticism virtually ignored it,[64] but later works by e.g. G. Pasquali[65] and M. L. West[66] have given it more appropriate treatment. Reynolds and Wilson caution us against extremes—particularly that of assuming that contamination is so rampant in textual

---

[59] See Tarrant 1995:108ff.

[60] See Reynolds 1983:435.

[61] Koester 1987:40–41.

[62] In the next chapter I discuss T. W. Allen's attempts at creating stemmata for the Homeric manuscript evidence.

[63] It should also be pointed out that papyri generally defy the whole concept of stemmatics, in that they invariably antedate the hypothetical archetype—which is usually presumed to date from the Byzantine period and to be the source of the medieval manuscript tradition.

[64] Maas 1958, English translation of his 1950 German edition.

[65] Pasquali 1952.

[66] West 1973.

traditions that the stemmatic method is of no use.[67] In the field of New Testament studies, the factor of contamination (or "conflation") was one of the three main reasons why Westcott and Hort removed from serious consideration the TR ("Textus Receptus") as a significant textual family (or, much less likely, as the original NT text). The TR, or "Syrian text-type," as they called it, was found to be full of "conflate" readings deriving from the two earlier text-types—the "Alexandrian" (which they, somewhat presumptuously, finally called "Neutral") and the "Western." As the Syrian readings were compared with those from the other two text-types, "their claim to be regarded as the original readings is found gradually to diminish, and at last to disappear."[68]

We have considered some of the issues which arise during the process of *recensio* and *emendatio*. At this point it would be well to step back and think more about the actual benefits of textual criticism, and to look at some examples. I refer to Martin West's book on textual criticism, where he discusses these benefits.[69] As I do so, I will be occasionally mentioning the situation regarding the text of Homer, with a view to discussing it in greater detail in the next chapter.

Firstly, and most obviously, textual criticism aims to allow us to determine (with a more or less reasonable degree of certainty) what precisely the author wrote.[70] Although this might seem natural and obvious enough, such precision can in fact have important consequences if the author was writing, for example, history or philosophy: there could be cases where the historicity, or at least important details, concerning a person, place, or battle hangs upon the veracity of a particular variant reading, or where a crucial thread of philosophical thought depends on ascertaining the precise wording of an argument. Details regarding economic situations or military events could even be obscured by confusion between letters, since letters of the alphabet were employed to represent numerals (in both Greek and Latin).

An example of this latter type of confusion occurs in Thucydides III 50.1. The manuscripts read χιλίων (1000), whereas a more "reasonable" number in the context would be τριάκοντα (30). Obviously it would be hard to see how corruption could have occurred if the words themselves were originally written; however if we allow that "one thousand" was represented

---

[67] Reynolds and Wilson 1991:288–289. They also here defend Maas (op. cit., n1) against the charge that he underestimated the importance of *contaminatio*. See also Tarrant 1995:108f.

[68] Quoted in Epp and Fee 1993:11–12.

[69] West 1973:7–9. As he himself states, his book improves on that of Maas (above, n1) in that it discusses contamination of manuscripts, which Maas had only briefly mentioned.

[70] See n1 above.

by the capital letter ‚A and "thirty" by Λ', the confusion is rather easier to understand.[71]

An historical example occurs in Herodotus VI 105–106, and concerns the name of the Athenian who ran to ask for help from the Spartans against the Persians (who had just landed at Marathon). Was his name Φιλιππίδης or Φειδιππίδης? Most modern editors print the former; although the manuscript evidence is less good than that for Φειδιππίδης, there is good support from other authors (Pausanius, Plutarch), and the name Φιλιππίδης is a common Athenian name. Φειδιππίδης, however, appears to be the humorous creation of Aristophanes (see *Clouds* 67), but it does have better manuscript authority; in addition it must be considered the *lectio difficilior* in this case (because of its comparative rarity, and, some have claimed, the inappropriateness of Aristophanes using in jest a name "consecrated in the tale of Marathon"; (but was he in fact constrained by any such scruples?), and therefore perhaps more likely to be the original reading. Without being certain as to which reading is genuine, one can easily see how one might have arisen from the other: when written in capitals, the letters Δ and Λ have become confused, along with the fact that the first syllables of each name (ει and ι) eventually came to be pronounced in the same way (itacism).[72] Of course such confusions, the first visual and the second audible, will also tell us something about the *date* at which (approximately) the error is most likely to have occurred: capital letters can obviously only be confused in an uncial manuscript (including papyri), while the convergence of the above vowel sounds occurred between the late classical and Byzantine periods. Thus we can say that this particular error most likely originated sometime between about the third and eighth centuries CE, before uncial manuscripts were superseded by minuscules.

The above example illustrates the weighing of the internal and external evidence, some consideration of the *lectio difficilior*, and an attempt to explain how one reading might have resulted from the other through confusion of script and phonology; despite these considerations, in this particular case one reading does not present itself as unmistakably "correct."

Needless to say, these types of copying errors (confusion of written letters, confusion of similar sounds) occur frequently in the transmission of the texts of all classical authors, and must not be ruled out in any examination of the text of Homer. However my claim will be that only *some* of the surviving variant readings in our text of Homer can be explained by invoking this sort of scribal error, and that in fact a significant number *cannot* be explained in this

---

[71] This example, and several others, are given in Reynolds and Wilson 1991:223–233.

[72] See a good discussion in Renehan 1969:68–69.

way; rather, the variants in question contain divergences so *substantial* and so *early*[73] that they lead one to conclude that there was no archetype in the usual sense.

To consider another example, we find in Plato's *Timaeus* an instance of significant variants in a philosophical passage. In 69–70 the soul, chest, and heart are being described; in 70A–B the following four variant readings occur, along with a scholarly conjecture:[74]

a) τὴν δὲ δὴ καρδίαν ἅμμα τῶν φλεβῶν ... κατέστησαν.
('the heart, the knot of the blood vessels ... they established') This is generally accepted as the correct reading; however the word ἅμμα is fairly rare and hence likely would have seemed unfamiliar to a scribe. This could explain a *conscious* change of the text.

b) τὴν δὲ δὴ καρδίαν ἅμα τῶν φλεβῶν ... κατέστησαν.
Assuming that the first reading is correct, this variant could have arisen *consciously*, as a scribe's replacement of the unfamiliar ἅμμα with the much more familiar ἅμα ('at the same time'). Or, treating it as an *unconscious* error, it could be explained as a case of haplography (accidentally writing one letter for two)—helped by the fact that the resultant word was indeed familiar. Alternatively, the reading could be due to the fact that in early uncial writing geminate consonants were as a rule written once only. However, when all is said and done, this reading gives an untranslatable clause. Renehan points out that Galen quotes this passage with this reading three times, indicating that the textual corruption is very early.[75]

c) τὴν δὲ δὴ καρδίαν ἀρχὴν ἅμα τῶν φλεβῶν ... κατέστησαν.
This reading, characterized as a Renaissance conjecture (it is found only in some later mss.), was occasioned presumably by the fact that Aristotle often calls the heart the ἀρχὴν τῶν φλεβῶν ('source of the blood vessels'); but of course the rationale behind the conjecture is to "correct" the unsyntactical ἅμα by supplying the missing antecedent for the genitive φλεβῶν.

d) ἄναμμα δὲ [sc. ὁ Πλάτων φησὶ] τῶν φλεβῶν τὴν καρδίαν ...
(ἄναμμα usually means 'ignited mass'; perhaps here 'attached knot') This is "Longinus"' paraphrase of the passage; note that he preserves evidence of the original reading. However when one weighs the manuscript evidence, this variant can be explained as an example of dittography—the accidental writing twice of something (in this case the two letters αν at the

---

[73] To use M. L. West's words (West 1973:41–42).
[74] See Renehan 1969:63–65.
[75] Ibid.

end of καρδίαν) which originally occurred only once: ΚΑΡΔΙΑΝΑΜΜΑ →
ΚΑΡΔΙΑΝΑΝΑΜΜΑ. Note that in the "Longinus" paraphrase the conditions for dittography are no longer apparent, since καρδίαν now no longer
precedes ἄναμμα; this means that the corruption must have antedated
him.

e)   τὴν δὲ δὴ καρδίαν ἀρχὴν νᾶμα τῶν φλεβῶν . . . κατέστησαν.
      This is a modern conjecture: indeed the conjectured word νᾶμα ('stream')
      occurs elsewhere in the *Timaeus* (and is frequent in Plato generally).
      However its meaning seems inappropriate in this passage.[76]

    This example illustrates several of the "canons" discussed above: the
preferring of the *lectio difficilior*, the fact that one can show how the true
reading was corrupted into one or more of the others (*utrum in alterum
abiturum erat?*[77]), and the non-acceptance of a conjecture if it does not actually improve the text. This much relates to internal evidence, and in this case
both transcriptional and intrinsic types come into play.[78] Additionally, the
weight assigned to external evidence plays a role, with the oldest manuscripts
preserving the genuine reading; choosing this correct reading is a rather
straightforward matter in this case.

    If the first benefit of doing textual criticism is to determine the actual
words of the author, then a second is that by closely examining and weighing
variant readings, one is led into a deeper knowledge of the author's style and
manner of thinking than might otherwise have been the case.[79] Merely to
ask such seemingly abstruse questions can lead to a close examination of an
author's style, and linguistic and (for poetry) metrical usage. Our knowledge
of his personal sensitivities may depend heavily upon the care with which
we weigh and decide between different readings. This can enrich our knowledge of the language itself, as well as of the relationships between authors of
the same and related genres. Conversely, of course, one's familiarity with an
author's style and content will enable him/her to make more informed decisions about what is the correct reading in cases where variants occur, and even
to detect cases of "corruption" where no variant readings have survived.[80]

    I have discussed how the editor of an ancient work must weigh both the
internal and the external evidence when deciding which variant to print in

---

[76] Ibid. In *Timaeus* 75E we find τὸ δὲ λόγων νᾶμα, 'the stream of speech'.
[77] See Appendix B.
[78] See above, p. 10, for the distinction.
[79] West 1973:8.
[80] Tarrant (1995:119) quotes D. R. Shackelton Bailey, who in describing the process of *emendatio*,
      mentions the "touchstones which knowledge and experience automatically apply."

the text, and which to relegate to the apparatus. Not infrequently there will be cases when *none* of the extant manuscripts gives a reading that can be considered original. Either there is one sole surviving reading which is patently incorrect, or two or more variants which are all faulty; or there may be a gap in the text (*lacuna*) which must be filled in order for the passage to make clear and coherent sense. There are also "borderline" cases, where the text before us *may* be correct as it is, but one or more scholars feel uncomfortable enough with it to propose their own replacement.

In each of the above cases, a "conjecture" may be proposed, the goal of which is to "repair" the text at the point at which it is evidently faulty; a conjecture which gains general acceptance then becomes known as an "emendation." The OED defines "conjecture" as "the proposal of a reading not actually found in the traditional text"; and "emendation" as "the correction (usually by conjecture or inference) of the text of an author where it is presumed to have been corrupted in transmission," and also "a textual alteration for this purpose."[81] In practice, however, the two terms are often interchanged, as well as sometimes being used in conjunction, viz. "conjectural emendation." One specialist puts it as follows: "If a conjecture is defined as a scholarly guess which attempts to improve the text at hand, then, strictly speaking, an emendation is a successful conjecture, one that actually removes a fault."[82] The art of conjecture was known as *divinatio* by the Romans, although as Tarrant notes, this term originally did not have mystic force but rather meant little more than guesswork.[83]

There is a range of views on how frequently conjecture should be applied, both in general and in specific cases; those writers who describe scholars at each end of the spectrum tend to excel in the use of both colorful and polemical language. For instance, those exhibiting one tendency have been described as "suffering from the occupational disease of the emendator—the final inability to leave well alone";[84] elsewhere this affliction is described as *pruritas emendandi*—the 'itch to emend'[85]; and Bentley, for whom emending texts was as natural as breathing, has been described as "wad[ing] knee-deep in the carnage of his emendations."[86]

---

[81] OED s.v. "conjecture" 4; "emendation" 2.b.
[82] Tarrant 1995:118. In a private communication he suggests that "emendations are conjectures that have been run up the flagpole and have garnered a sizable number of salutes."
[83] Ibid.
[84] Quoted in Renehan 1969:104.
[85] Metzger 1992:184.
[86] Strugnell 1974:543.

The opposite extreme is found in the case of most NT textual critics. Bentley himself is quoted as admitting that "in the sacred text . . . there is no place for conjecture or emendation," although later he says he will add any such proposals separately in his *Prologomena*.[87] Other scholars seem to have come to the consensus that there is such an abundance of textual evidence that the original reading must survive somewhere, and it is the textual critic's task to locate and print it. This is sometimes accompanied by the theological belief that Providence would have preserved the sacred text without allowing a single original reading to be lost. One New Testament scholar cites the view that in dealing with the text of the New Testament conjecture tends to become "a process precarious in the extreme, and seldom allowing anyone but the guesser to feel confidence in the truth of its results."[88] Metzger lays down such stringent requirements for a successful conjecture that the most likely one in the New Testament, in 1 Peter 3:19, fails in spite of its many attractions.[89] Such conservatism may arise less from a "distrust of critical judgment,"[90] than from a feeling of reverence toward the text, based on the premise of divine inspiration.

A further New Testament example occurs in 2 Peter 3.10. Many variants are recorded, none of which seems to be "original."[91] The verse is dealing with the future apocalyptic destruction of the earth. The verse concludes:

καὶ γῆ καὶ τὰ ἐν αὐτῇ ἔργα <u>εὑρεθήσεται</u>.

. . . and the earth and the works in it <u>shall be found</u>.

Clearly something is not quite right here, although this reading has the best ancient external evidence in its favor. One early papyrus adds the word λυόμενα 'dissolved'—except that the verb λύω is already used twice in the immediate context. Other ancient variants include ἀφανισθήσονται 'will disappear' and κατακαήσεται 'will be burned up'. In addition scholars have conjectured the following:

πυρωθήσεται 'will be burned'
ἐκπυρωθήσεται 'will be burnt to ashes'

---

[87] Strugnell 1974:543.

[88] Greenlee 1964:15, quoting Frederic G. Kenyon.

[89] Mss. ἐν ᾧ καί; conjectures: Ενωχ [Enoch] καί and ἐν ᾧ καὶ Ενωχ; see Metzger 1971:693; also Metzger 1992:182–185. "[The successful conjecture] must not just satisfy the tests of the correct variant, but it must satisfy them absolutely well . . . its fitness [must be] exact and perfect . . . The only criterion of a successful conjecture is that it shall approve itself as inevitable."

[90] See n38 above.

[91] Metzger 1971:705–706.

ἀρθήσεται 'will be taken away' and
κριθήσεται 'will be judged'.

However none of these is printed in the Greek text—it is left with the virtually meaningless εὑρεθήσεται.

A corrective to this "hyper-conservative" view is achieved when we realize that one of its motivations really does appear to be a basic distrust of human critical judgment—the underlying and perhaps unconscious assumption that somehow anything that is "ancient" or even "old" is somehow bound to be more reliable than someone's intelligent surmise. Tanselle stresses that the process of *recensio* is just as conjectural as that of *emendatio* (he appears to include *examinatio* as a part of *recensio*)—both procedures are based completely on human judgment.[92] Thus just as a recension can be good or bad, so can a conjecture. For an example of an unnecessary and indeed inappropriate conjecture, see the example from Plato's *Timaeus* above.[93]

An example of a necessary and satisfying conjecture involves Housman's emendation of Martial (*Liber Spectaculorum* 21.8)[94]:

haec tamen res est facta ita pictoria   (mss.)
haec tantum res est facta παρ' ἱστορίαν.   (Housman)

'This thing alone happened contrary to the story.'

The confusion of the last two words arose from misreading the Greek uncials as Latin:

ΠΑΡΙⳞΤΟΡΙΑ   →   ΙΤΑΡΙCΤΟRΙΑ

This conjecture is all the more satisfying because it neatly fulfills the transcriptional requirement—that the correct reading be able to account for the origin of the corrupt reading. And of course it makes excellent sense—as well as possessing the "learned" feature of a Greek quote in the midst of a Latin poem.

An enlightening (and humorous) account of how one scholar has made conjectures in Latin literature is provided by Robin Nisbet.[95] In his article Nisbet contrasts the need to "fiddle with the letters" in order to determine what the original must have been,[96] with the frequent need to "clutch out of

---

[92] Tanselle 1995:20.
[93] Pp. 19–20.
[94] See Renehan 1969:46–47. The actor playing Orpheus was killed by a bear during a performance of the Orpheus legend.
[95] Nisbet 1991.
[96] Ibid., 72.

the air a word with perhaps no more than a general resemblance to the transmitted reading."[97]

A New Testament scholar, John Strugnell,[98] some years ago reacted against the entrenched conservative tendencies of his colleagues with an article entitled "A Plea for Conjectural Emendation in the New Testament."[99] In this article Strugnell critically examines the reasons why NT scholars have been and continue to be so reticent about making or accepting conjectures into their editions of the NT text. Such reasons include the following: there is such a vast amount of evidence that the correct reading must survive somewhere ("wishful thinking"), the comparative excellence of the manuscripts (this is a *petitio principii*, i.e. an example of circular reasoning), the relative antiquity of manuscripts (but what about an early corruption that has affected the archetype?), and the belief that the archetype is identical to the autograph (an assumption that can never be proved).

Strugnell even suggests that it may at times be necessary to "correct the author himself"—a suggestion which runs counter to most editors, especially those of biblical texts.[100] He divides errors into two types: those of the author and those made subsequently—but of course we can never be sure which is which.[101] And each type is open to conjectural emendation if we are dissatisfied with the text as it stands.

Strugnell's "plea" was answered by a fellow NT scholar, G. D. Kilpatrick, in 1981.[102] Kilpatrick, who does not appear to be against conjecture for the reasons given above, nevertheless is uncomfortable with Strugnell's readiness to correct the author, and to the consequent opening the door to "considerable rewriting of the New Testament."[103] In addition Kilpatrick suggests that the true dichotomy is not between conjectures and manuscript readings, for certainly some readings, even ancient ones, are themselves conjectures (presumably made by scribes); but between conjectures and non-conjectures.[104] He distin-

---

[97] Ibid., 66. On p. 91 he suggests that, for making conjectures, "The period after Christmas is particularly productive, when everything is shut and one is slouched in an arm-chair half-asleep."

[98] Strugnell was also heavily involved with the original editing and publishing of the Dead Sea Scrolls.

[99] Strugnell 1974.

[100] Cf. the precept that an editor "will not hesitate to correct the archetype but never venture to correct the author," quoted in Tarrant 1995:118.

[101] Renehan (1969:22–23) gives an example from Eustathius where he thinks it quite possible that the error originated with the author.

[102] Kilpatrick 1981.

[103] Ibid., 357–358.

[104] Ibid.

guishes between conjecture and deliberate change (by scribes) and character-izes a non-conjecture as a reading which, although not the original reading, is nevertheless derived from or a part of the transmitted text; while a conjecture, though "related" to the text, is not part of this transmitted text, nor derived from it.[105] He thus contrasts the uncertainty inherent in the (perhaps inspired) guesswork of the conjecture with the (implied) certainty of the transmitted text, and thus seems to be falling into the trap of allowing anything old to be of greater value than a modern intelligent and educated conjecture. I note that in the same volume in which Kilpatrick's article appears there is also a paper discussing how modern translations of the New Testament deal with the problem of a corrupt text.[106] It appears that although a conjecture sometimes must be made in order to have a sensible English translation, nevertheless the conservatism of biblical editors keeps them from actually introducing many such conjectures into editions of their Greek texts.[107]

This degree of conservatism is rarely apparent among editors of clas-sical texts.[108] Indeed, the earlier extreme divergence of opinions and the accompanying mutual hostility has, according to Richard Tarrant, in the past achieved "almost grotesque proportions" but has more recently settled into a calmer state.[109] Editors are now sometimes classified as "conservative" (more likely to follow the transmitted text) or "skeptical" (more inclined to emend the text)[110]; the ideal is said to be that balance of conservatism and skepti-cism which leads one to "be as ready to preserve the transmitted text when it is sound as to emend it when it is defective."[111] This ideal includes warnings against supposing that the transmitted text is only faulty when it is obviously so, balanced with the necessity of only altering an archetype when there is good reason to do so.[112] Tarrant further describes this optimal methodology negatively: not "is what we have intelligible?" (conservative), nor "is what we have the best conceivable?" (skeptical), but "is what we have the words in which this author would likely have expressed this meaning?"[113] Accurately

---

[105] Ibid., 358–359.

[106] Rhodes 1981.

[107] See above, pp. 24–25.

[108] Although Nisbet (1991:88) imagines that his conservative critics may accuse him of *cacoethes coniciendi*, which phrase then leads him to make a further conjecture.

[109] Tarrant 1995:119–120.

[110] Tarrant 1989:124 cites the extreme case of an editor of Euripides who, in his readiness to excise supposedly "interpolated" lines, worked "on a principle somewhat like that of the provincial English dentist—'if you won't miss it, why not have it out?' "

[111] Ibid.

[112] Ibid.

[113] Ibid.

answering this last question naturally requires a deep familiarity with the author's style and patterns of thought, for which no mechanical shortcuts or formulaic approaches can substitute.[114]

I close this brief discussion on conjecture by mentioning that one of the most prolific and influential Homeric scholars of the past generation, M. van der Valk, has written frequently that the Alexandrian scholars who worked on the text of Homer, i.e. Zenodotus, Aristophanes, and Aristarchus, made their alterations to the Homeric text not by choosing one variant out of several which appeared in the manuscripts available to them, but rather by basing their decision on subjective reasons such as what is "appropriate"; they were merely "rewriting" Homer according to their own personal preferences. In the preface to his 1949 work on the Odyssey, van der Valk states bluntly that "the ancient critics are not to be trusted and have altered the original text in many places by making subjective conjectures."[115]

In the next chapter I shall examine the different ways in which textual criticism has been applied to the Homeric text; I shall argue that the regular rules of textual criticism do not always "work" when dealing with Homer. I will also suggest that the Alexandrian scholars, far from exercising the kind of capricious subjectivity alleged by van der Valk, instead used manuscript evidence and an intelligent and educated sense of judgment in much the same way that a modern editor does. The question to be considered there will be: what is the significance both of the quantity, and more importantly of the quality, of the variant readings which have survived as witnesses to the text of Homer?

---

[114] Nisbet (op. cit.) exemplifies this familiarity with his authors, as does Housman (op. cit.).

[115] Van der Valk 1949:9. The phrase "subjective conjecture" is one of his favorites.

Chapter 2

Homer and Textual Criticism

AVING EXAMINED AND DISCUSSED THE VARIOUS PRINCIPLES used in editing classical and biblical texts, I turn my attention to the specific case of Homer.[1] My argument will be that since Homer is different from other classical texts, we cannot simply apply the canons of textual criticism to the surviving manuscripts of the *Iliad* and *Odyssey*. I recall my introductory remarks, where I stressed the need to consider not only the evidence but also the theory;[2] many scholars pay lip-service to the theory of oral composition and transmission for the purposes of literary analysis and criticism, but then when they look at the Homeric textual evidence they tend to treat it in much the same way as they would that of Apollonius Rhodius or some other poet who wrote.[3]

There are even those who envision Homer as a sort of literary collector and combiner of myths, traditions, and geographical details, who has already made choices between variant readings for us. All we need to do, it is supposed, is to find out exactly what he wrote down, and then we will have the "real Homer," in the same way as we might have the "real Virgil."[4] I compare the way in which Elias Lönnrot, in compiling what is known as the *Kalevala*, a collection of epic material from various parts of Finland, "merged variants of songs from different regions"; and further "had access to manuscript collections containing variants of songs from various regions ... and he chose elements from those variants."[5] Here we see a literate scholar surveying the

---

[1]   This chapter is a significantly expanded version of a previous article, Bird 1994.
[2]   See Introduction.
[3]   An exception is P. von der Muehll: in the preface to his 1962 edition of the *Odyssey* he writes: "cum inane videatur etiam in Homero ut in ceteris scriptoribus edendis unum quasi verum textum legentibus obtrudere, restat, ut diversae lectiones ... iuxta exhibeantur." In contrast, most editors of Homer appear content to "force" upon their readers their idea of the "one true text."
[4]   See e.g. Taplin 1986.
[5]   See Lord 1991:106. Magoun (1963:351) states that Lönnrot had determined that variants of the same song should be woven into one song and not published separately.

widely varying material and himself making the decisions as to what, on the one hand, achieves canonicity or authenticity, and what is rejected—just like the modern editor of a written work.

It is the purpose of this chapter to show that the variation in our surviving manuscripts of Homer (and other sources) is inconsistent with a single archetype, but rather points back to a multiplicity of archetypes, a situation which arises from the oral nature of the transmission of Homeric epic. By attempting to follow the traditional text-critical techniques illustrated in the previous chapter, it will become apparent that such a methodology breaks down in the case of Homer. And unlike the case with Virgil's *Aeneid*, it will not be contamination alone which prevents the creation of a neat stemma—contamination merely being (as stated above) the *horizontal* influence between manuscripts; nor is it merely the *quantity* of manuscripts of Homer which leads to this conclusion, but also their *quality*—i.e. the degree to which they diverge from any kind of "norm," whether it be the "vulgate" or other traditional standard; these divergences occur in ways which can be characterized neither as *horizontal* nor as *vertical* influence.

I began the previous chapter with this statement: "The primary goal of textual criticism has traditionally been to establish the actual text that the author wrote, so far as this is possible."[6] In working with Homer, one immediately runs into problems with the formulation "the actual text which the author wrote," in particular with the very concept of an "author" and the idea that he "wrote" anything.[7] The fact that there are difficulties even in expressing the purported goal of textual criticism (except for those few scholars who believe Homer actually did sit down and write the *Iliad* and *Odyssey* in much the same way that Virgil wrote the *Aeneid*) should make us cautious as we think about applying this goal and its methods to the extant manuscripts of Homer.

An associated benefit of textual criticism discussed above is that it enables us to learn more about Homer's style, language, and poetic (including metrical) usage.[8] In the case of Homer, the term "style" includes the concept of the "formula"; and we shall see that in the context of "formulaic" material the very concept of "variant" needs to be redefined.[9]

---

[6] See n1 in chap. 1.
[7] Nagy (1996b:19–27) warns against statements of the form "Homer + [verb]" (p. 20) and especially "Homer wrote" (p. 27).
[8] See West 1973:8, and the previous chapter of this book.
[9] See Lord 1960. On p. 101 Lord states that strictly speaking, "we cannot speak of a 'variant'—there is no 'original' to be varied!"

If we have learned anything from the work of Milman Parry[10] and Albert Lord,[11] it is at least this: that epic poetry in the Troy tradition was performed orally long before any part of what we now know as the *Iliad* and *Odyssey* was ever written down, and that no one of these oral performances was identical to any other; hence no one performance—or any written record of it—could lay claim to possessing ultimate and unique authority as being the "original version" of the *Iliad* or *Odyssey* (it seems that only with the appearance of the "vulgate"did any such authoritativeness become attached to a written text of Homer). Each time an ἀοιδός ('performer of Homeric epic poetry') sang his song, it was a unique and "original" performance, yet one firmly rooted in tradition, inasmuch as it was expressed by means of traditional language and themes. I offer this typical quotation from Parry:

> No singer ever tells the same tale twice in the same words. His poem will always follow the same general pattern, but this verse or that will be left out, or replaced by another verse or part of a verse, and he will leave out and add whole passages as the time and the mood of his hearers calls for a fuller or a briefer telling of a tale or of a given part of a tale. Thus the oral poem even in the mouth of the same singer is ever in a state of change; and it is the same when his poetry is sung by others.[12]

Lord too would have us get away from the idea of an "original" text: "From one point of view each performance is an original"; "each performance is . . . a re-creation"; "each performance is 'an' original, if not 'the' original"; and finally "the author of an oral epic . . . is the performer."[13]

Thus if more than one of these performances were to be recorded in writing, we would expect to find texts of Homer that differed significantly from one another, more so than surviving texts of originally written works such as Virgil's *Aeneid*. And unlike the situation with Virgil, one particular Homeric manuscript would therefore not necessarily be derived from another through the process of copying and the inevitable errors associated with scribal activities. Rather, a manuscript of Homer could be derived from an oral performance which was more or less different from any other performance, thus giving rise to "variants" which would be inexplicable if one were to depend solely on the canons of textual criticism as applied to written works.

[10]   Parry 1971.
[11]   Lord 1960.
[12]   Parry 1971:336.
[13]   Lord 1960:100–101.

I am not completely ruling out the existence of scribal errors in our texts of Homer—indeed such errors do occur both in Homeric papyri and in the medieval manuscripts of Homer (although the type of analysis I am here arguing for makes it more difficult to simply write off any given variant as an "error"). Rather I am proposing to treat in a special way variant readings of the type which "differ markedly from the traditional text in a way which cannot be explained by the processes of merely mechanical corruption."[14] I plan to do this by giving such variants the benefit of the doubt, as it were, and not automatically assuming that one reading is right and all others are wrong, as would be reasonable in the case of the text of, say, Virgil's *Aeneid*.[15]

As far as manuscript evidence is concerned, what survives in the case of Homer is firstly, as mentioned briefly in the previous chapter, the large number of (mostly fragmentary) papyri from the Ptolemaic, Roman, and Byzantine periods,[16] and secondly, the sizeable collection of medieval manuscripts—fewer in number than the papyri but generally containing a far greater quantity of text, and in much better physical condition. We also have the indirect evidence of the scholia, as well as quotations from ancient authors such as Aeschines and Plato. Finally there is the evidence of early inscriptions and vase paintings.[17] When it comes to agreement with the "vulgate,"[18] it is the earliest papyri—those from the Ptolemaic period—which show the most significant divergences, while the later medieval manuscripts differ much less from our "modern" text (e.g. the OCT). The other types of evidence (inscriptions and iconographic objects) are also more likely, the older they are, to contain significant deviations from the "received text" (an equivalent term for "vulgate"), often preserving readings (and versions of episodes, if we include the evidence of vase painting) as "wild" as those of the earliest Ptolemaic papyri.[19] As time

---

[14] S. West 1967:11, with reference to the variants in the Ptolemaic papyri.

[15] West (2001:162) appears to agree, stressing the need to "consider all variants on their merits"; he is particularly opposed to the approach of editors such as H. van Thiel, who ignores variants from papyri, quotations, and readings attributed to ancient Homeric scholars such as Aristarchus.

[16] I roughly date the three periods as follows: Ptolemaic: 3rd–1st centuries BCE; Roman: 1st–3rd centuries CE; Byzantine: 4th–8th centuries CE. See chap. 3 below, on the Ptolemaic papyri. I also point out there the convention whereby some non-papyrus manuscripts are nevertheless labeled as if they were on papyrus.

[17] See Nagy 1996b:67f. Also Snodgrass 1998.

[18] By "vulgate" I mean the reading of the majority of medieval manuscripts; Haslam (1997:63) stresses that the term "designates no particular version of the text"; on pp. 84f. he has an informative discussion on the vexed question of the origin of the vulgate.

[19] See Snodgrass 1998:118–120 for an example of a vase depicting the Funeral Games for Patroklos; the depiction agrees with our *Iliad* XXIII in several features, but differs in others, notably the fact that Diomedes takes third place in the chariot race, whereas in the *Iliad* he is the winner.

passes, the frequency and the extent of textual and other variation diminish; in fact there is a distinct terminus at around 150 BCE. This date is presumed roughly to coincide with the end of the editorial work of the greatest of the Alexandrian textual scholars, Aristarchus of Samothrace (ca. 216–144 BCE),[20] thanks to whom, apparently, the "eccentric" variations were largely eliminated from subsequent texts of Homer.[21] I observe at this point that the way in which the Alexandrian scholars carried out their textual work (in particular the reasons behind some of their editorial decisions) is somewhat unclear to us; modern scholars can be quick to label a reading of, say, Zenodotus as a conjecture,[22] whereas a more careful examination of the evidence illustrates that these earliest "editors" of the Homeric text were often more scholarly than we give them credit for.[23] The problem is that almost none of their textual readings found their way into the later manuscripts, an issue which will be discussed below.

In the case of a written text, one tends to find the opposite situation from what exists for Homer. For example, for the text of Virgil's *Aeneid* there are seven manuscripts dating from the fourth to the sixth centuries, and a mass of medieval manuscripts starting in the late eighth and early ninth century. The older witnesses are considered more trustworthy and authentic, and are "the editor's mainstay,"[24] whereas it is the later ones which contain more significant and complicated deviations from the "standard" text. The conventional theory behind such a state of affairs is that over the passage of time, errors gradually creep into a text as it is copied and recopied; the details of this process were discussed in the previous chapter. Such errors can arise inadvertently, or they may result from a deliberate decision to alter the current text. An example of the latter in the *Aeneid* is book II, lines 567–588; these lines are not in any of the best and oldest manuscripts. Either they did originally belong in the text, and were deleted as reflecting badly on Aeneas, or they were added later, in

---

An alternative explanation cited (disapprovingly) by Snodgrass for the discrepancy is that "Kleitias [the painter] could not remember the field." See also Nagy 1996b:107.

[20] Pfeiffer 1968:211.

[21] S. West 1967:16. T. W. Allen claims to have invented the use of the term "eccentric" to describe the Ptolemaic papyri; see Allen 1924:302.

[22] I refer again to van der Valk 1949:9 (cited in chap. 1 n115): "[T]he ancient critics are not to be trusted and have altered the original text in many places by making subjective conjectures." He frequently uses the phrase "subjective conjecture" (or some variant of it) in his dismissal of the work of Zenodotus et al.

[23] See for example Nickau 1977. Other scholars who are not so quick to disparage the work of the Alexandrians include Ludwich (1898), Allen (1924), Bolling (1925 and 1944), Apthorp (1980), and Nagy (1996a and 2004).

[24] Reynolds 1983:433.

order to fill a perceived lacuna in the narrative. There is presently no scholarly consensus on the question of their genuineness; from the point of view of establishing the "original text" they are either genuine or they are not.[25] Typically of most classical works, the earliest manuscripts of the *Aeneid* are the most reliable in establishing the "true text." The later manuscripts tend to be so corrupted with errors, many of which arise from contamination as different readings are compared and collated, that their usefulness is significantly reduced. In the case of the text of the *Aeneid*, the complex medieval manuscript tradition makes it hard to see the wood for the trees.[26] With Homer, as noted above, the reverse is the case: it is the *earliest* witnesses to the text which contain the most divergent readings, while the later manuscripts tend to converge toward the "received text."

In order to properly comprehend this state of affairs, we need to return to Parry and Lord's fundamental findings about oral traditional poetry. As Parry himself said in 1932,

> One thing is plain: our manuscripts cannot all go back to a manuscript of Homer's time; for their variant readings, while some are due to copyists, are for the greater part the variants of an oral tradition, which means that the manuscripts which the Alexandrians used came from different oral traditions.[27]

Apparently this prospect is unsettling to some scholars. M. van der Valk feels that if the Homeric text was transmitted originally orally, and was thus exposed to various "vicissitudes and alterations," then one must accept that "[i]t was so to speak in a state of continuous evolution and metamorphosis. It is obvious that the acceptance of this theory has far-reaching consequences. The whole basis of our Homeric text becomes uncertain."[28] It is as if we lose

---

[25] Compare the four lines in *Iliad* IX 458–461 (from the speech of Phoenix): these lines are preserved by Plutarch, occur in no extant manuscript, and were reportedly omitted by Aristarchus φοβειθείς 'out of fear'. Bolling (1925:120–122) judges these lines to be interpolations, but most editors print them, rather than relegating them to the apparatus. West (2001:208) calls them "uncanonical" but in his 1998 edition encloses them within a special type of marker (⌊ ⌋) which he does not explain, rather than the usual braces ({}) to indicate interpolation. Evidently the lines, although "weakly attested," are too good to throw away.

[26] Reynolds 1983:435. Note the reference to *silva immensa*, regarding the inextricably intertwined mass of manuscripts, a situation that does not allow for the creation of a satisfactory stemma.

[27] *Harvard Studies in Classical Philology* 43 (1932), pp. 46–47 = *MHV* p. 361.

[28] van der Valk 1964:266–267. In n13 he says, "I cannot imagine that the theory of alterations of the text by rhapsodes might be applied to the Homeric text." This sounds more like an emotional reaction than a conclusion based upon a judicious consideration of the evidence. Cf. p. 373: "The idea of interpolation by rhapsodes would be very acceptable, if the Homeric text

"our" *Iliad* and *Odyssey*, and even "our Homer"; in exchange we get something that lacks the kind of stability to which we are accustomed; instead of a poet whom we can admire we get a tradition consisting of many anonymous poets. And yet, a proper understanding of oral-traditional poetry should lead us to feel that we have gained, rather than lost, as we look again at the Homeric text, freeing ourselves from the shackles of anachronistic assumptions regarding written transmission and all that follows from them.[29]

Other scholars, though more objective in their approach than van der Valk, still see no necessary connection between the unusual variants of the "eccentric" papyri and the nature of oral tradition.[30] It comes back to viewing the evidence in the light of a clear understanding of oral poetry and how it is composed, performed, and transmitted.

I cite two biblical analogies, although neither is an exact parallel, inasmuch as neither involves oral transmission in anything similar to the Homeric situation. The Dead Sea Scrolls, first discovered in 1947, gave scholars manuscripts of the Hebrew Bible (among other works) which pre-dated the earliest existing texts by at least a thousand years. A few conservative writers (theologically speaking) were quick to point out that the small differences between, say, the Isaiah scroll and the Massoretic text of Isaiah were so small as to inspire confidence in the belief that the Hebrew text had been transmitted "essentially unchanged" since its original putting down in writing. Others, however, looked at these same "small differences" and were able to show that there must at that time have existed differing texts of the book of Isaiah, and furthermore that each of these texts could be assigned a different geographical location, the so-called theory of "local texts."[31] Similarly, and with an appreciation of the differing situations, I suggest that we need to look at all Homeric textual variations, whether they appear "significant" or "insignificant," and

---

had been transmitted orally ... however ... I tried to show that this view must be dismissed." And this is thirty years after Parry!

[29] Nagy (1996b:111–112) contrasts losing "a historical author whom we never knew anyway" with recovering "a mythical author who is more than just an author ... who will come back to life with every performance of his *Iliad* and *Odyssey*." Cf. Nagy 1996a:152: "If you accept the reality of multiforms, you forfeit the elusive certainty of finding the original composition of Homer but you gain ... another certainty ... you recover a significant portion of the Homeric repertoire."

[30] S. West 1967:13: "The relatively minor scale of the interpolations argues against the view that there is a connection between the eccentricities of the early texts and the long oral tradition of the poems, except in so far as the rather discursive style suitable for oral technique attracted interpolation." The phrase "rather discursive style suitable for oral technique" seems to me to significantly mischaracterize the nature of oral composition in performance.

[31] Cross 1992: chap. 11.

understand them in the light of the nature of the poetry with which we are dealing.

The second parallel is in the field of New Testament textual criticism. E. J. Epp, in reflecting on the future of the discipline, writes that "we need to face the complex and perhaps unsettling notion of *multivalence* in the term *original text*. In other words, the issue is more difficult, has wider implications, and is also richer and potentially more rewarding than we might have imagined."[32] He continues "there is a real sense in which every intentional, meaningful scribal alteration to a text . . . creates a new Textform, a new original."[33] If instead of the words "scribal alteration to a text" we read "performance variation," we can almost hear the voice of Albert Lord.[34] Epp concludes by repeating his phrase "*multivalence of the term 'original' text*" and by adding the further suggestive words "*dimensions of originality*."[35]

As discussed above and in the previous chapter, when one is dealing with a text which was written down as it was composed, whenever a variant occurs it is usually (but not always) possible to choose one reading as original, and the other as a corruption of it (for example by the theory of the *lectio difficilior*). One is thus justified in distinguishing between the "genuine" and the "spurious" readings. With Homer, I shall be considering variant readings, *each* of which appears as "genuine" and "authentic" as the others; in these cases by comparing and weighing both internal and external evidence,[36] I hope to show that neither variant can be shown to be *the* correct reading—rather *both* can be considered "correct." Thus I will use terms such as "authentic," "original," "genuine," etc., to characterize readings which appear to be Homeric in both nature and lineage, but not in order to rule out other readings as "spurious" or "inauthentic." For the same reasons I shall avoid using such terms as "superior" and "inferior."[37]

As an example of what I suggest is a more appropriate way of dealing with variant readings in Homer, I consider the very beginning of the *Iliad* (I leave out for the moment the fact that according to the A scholia Zenodotus athetised these two lines).

ἡρώων, αὐτοὺς δὲ ἑλώρια τεῦχε κύνεσσιν
οἰωνοῖσί τε πᾶσι, Διὸς δ' ἐτελείετο βουλή,

---

[32] Epp 2002:72; his emphasis.
[33] Ibid., 74–75.
[34] Lord 1960:100.
[35] Epp 2002:75, his emphasis.
[36] See Appendix B for definitions of terms.
[37] Cf. Nagy 1996a:118, 133, 146, who prefers terms such as "traditional" to "superior."

... of heroes, and made them prey for dogs
and all birds, and the will of Zeus was being fulfilled ...

Iliad I 4–5, "vulgate"

Zenodotus (according to Athenaeus 12F) read:

ἡρώων, αὐτοὺς δὲ ἑλώρια τεῦχε κύνεσσιν
οἰωνοῖσί τε δαῖτα, Διὸς δ' ἐτελείετο βουλή,

... of heroes, and made them prey for dogs
and for birds food, and the will of Zeus was being fulfilled ...

I start by looking at various types of internal evidence in support of each reading. One immediately notices that Zenodotus' text presents a neater parallel between lines 4 and 5: a chiastic arrangement involving accusative-dative-dative-accusative: 'prey for dogs and for birds food'. It also gives line 5 a great deal more alliterative effect—note the preponderance of dental stops (including dental nasal 'n', as also in line 4):

οἰ<u>ω</u>νοῖσί <u>τ</u>ε <u>δ</u>αῖ<u>τ</u>α, Διὸς <u>δ</u>' ἐ<u>τ</u>ελείε<u>τ</u>ο βουλή,

Much of this effect is lost by the removal of δαῖτα in the "vulgate" rendering. Now a conventional textual critic might be inclined to reject Zenodotus' reading precisely because of the "nicer" parallel it offers between lines 4 and 5, as well as the alliteration in line 5; the reasoning would be that if δαῖτα were "original," no scribe would deliberately remove it and replace it with πᾶσι, a reading which destroys the parallel chiastic construction and undermines the alliterative force of line 5. In other words, the vulgate's *lectio difficilior* must be original, since one can easily understand how it was changed into Zenodotus' *lectio facilior*, while a change in the opposite direction is much harder to explain.

On the other hand, the "usual" reading πᾶσι has its own internal support. It can be shown to be formulaic[38] in this position[39] (as indeed can δαῖτα—cf. *Iliad* I 424); also it provides a less obvious (and hence more subtle) balance between the two phrases—i.e. not the simple chiastic structure of the reading with δαῖτα. In addition, Nagy adduces the concept of "hyperbolic allness," found in such passages as *Iliad* V 52 and *Odyssey* xviii 85, as support for the "vulgate" reading.[40]

[38] By "formulaic" here I mean that a specific word or phrase occurs in the same metrical position in at least one other line of Homer.
[39] Cf. *Odyssey* xvii 213; also compare ... πᾶσα Διὸς ... in *Odyssey* xii 416 and xiv 306.
[40] Nagy 1996a:134–135.

So much for *internal* evidence. In terms of *external* evidence (manuscript or other testimonial support) δαῖτα, while it lacks *quantity* of manuscript support, nevertheless makes up for it in *age*: when we consider the evidence of Aeschylus in the *Suppliants*, lines 800–801,[41] it becomes likely that he had access to a version of *Iliad* book one which had δαῖτα rather than πᾶσι. I note further, following Nagy,[42] that the term "version" here would refer to the performance tradition rather than the manuscript tradition, in other words that Aeschylus will have heard a performance of this part of the *Iliad* which included δαῖτα. Thus this reading can be dated back into the first half of the fifth century. The "vulgate" reading πᾶσι has (by definition) the overwhelming support of the manuscript tradition.

So far we have seen that both readings have both internal and external support. Therefore I would claim that both can be considered to be "genuine." Both fit well in context, and each has an ancient tradition behind it. However, traditional text-critical thinking, divorced from the realities of oral performance and transmission, forces scholars to make a choice. We can compare various opinions about the two readings: Pfeiffer[43] thinks that Zenodotus' δαῖτα is the genuine original reading, which Aristarchus replaced with his own πᾶσι. Kirk,[44] on the other hand, sees πᾶσι as authentic, and, without giving any reasons, characterizes Zenodotus' δαῖτα as "a fussy change of the vulgate." Similarly van der Valk[45] describes the reading of Zenodotus as "a subjective conjecture." However van der Valk also explicitly states as "absurd" the possibility that Aeschylus and Sophocles had access to (written) texts of Homer, which contained respectively the readings inherited by Zenodotus and the vulgate.[46] Since he cannot accept the consequences such a view would entail, he necessarily must reject it out of hand.[47] However, to repeat, my point is that if we look closely at the internal and external evidence for each reading, we shall find that both of them have good evidence in their support.[48] There is no need to choose one reading and reject the other (apart from the editorial requirements of privileging one reading at the expense of all others[49]): problems arise when we treat the Homeric material as if it were a fixed written

---

[41] κυσὶν δ' ἔπειθ' ἕλωρα κἀπιχωρίοις ὄρνισι / δεῖπνον οὐκ ἀναίνομαι πέλειν.
[42] Nagy 1996a:134n119.
[43] Pfeiffer 1968:113.
[44] Kirk 1985:53.
[45] van der Valk 1964:68.
[46] Ibid.
[47] Ibid. for a list of other scholars for and against each reading.
[48] See esp. Pfeiffer 1968:111ff.
[49] Standard editions of Homer have little choice but to do this; a "multitext" edition would allow the presentation of multiple variants without favoring one over the others.

text.[50] West characterizes Zenodotus' δαῖτα as "apparently a variant familiar to Aeschylus . . . but that does not make it *the original* reading; πᾶσι is good idiom" [my emphasis].[51]

Still on the same passage, I note the comments of Walter Leaf in his commentary, which pre-dates Parry by several decades. Leaf describes πᾶσι as "a perfectly natural expression." As for Zenodotus' reading, it is only in Athenaeus, "on whom no reliance can be placed." However the reading is in itself "vigorous and poetical." Leaf thinks that "the metaphor is so natural that we cannot even argue with confidence that Aeschylus (*Supp.* 800) had δαῖτα before him when he wrote." But after mentioning passages from Euripides (*Hec.* 1077, *Ion* 505), and Sophocles (*Ajax* 830), he concludes that "in all these cases there is an apparent echo of the present passage, and δαῖτα if a real variant is much older than Zenodotus." "On the whole δαῖτα seems intrinsically a better reading, but we have no right to leave the uniform tradition of the mss."[52] Perhaps this scholar, if he had lived to benefit from Parry's researches, would have agreed that in a case like this, where two variants both have legitimate claims to authenticity, the best treatment is one which grants such authenticity to both readings. In the words of a post-Parryan scholar, "Both variants are traditional multiforms. In a multitext format of editing Homer, we would have to take both forms into account."[53]

While we are in the proem of the *Iliad*, I note that there are other significant textual variations which deserve consideration; I mention two of them briefly here.

i) πολλὰς δ' ἰφθίμους ψυχὰς Ἄϊδι προΐαψεν,

And it [i.e. the Wrath of Achilles] hurled many strong souls down
      to Hades . . .

Iliad I 3 ("vulgate")

πολλὰς δ' ἰφθίμους κεφαλὰς Ἄϊδι προΐαψεν,

And it hurled many strong heads down to Hades . . .

Apollonius Rhodius,[54] also κακῶς τινες 'some very poor copies'[55]

---

[50] I also note the scholiastic comment that δαῖτα is never used for the food of animals in Homer, whereas it is in fact so used at *Iliad* XXIV 43.

[51] West 2001:173.

[52] Leaf 1902:3–4.

[53] Nagy 1996a:134. Finkelberg (2000:1–11) sees multiformity in the Cyclic epics, but considers the evidence insufficient to justify applying the term "multiformity" to the Homeric texts; she instead argues for treating them in the same way as regular written texts, including the use of such terms as "emendation" and "interpolation."

[54] According to a scholion to the T manuscript of the *Iliad*.

[55] Schol. A^im—i.e. Aristonicus, according to Erbse (1969:7). "A^im" indicates a scholion in the

Compare:

πολλὰς ἰφθίμους <u>κεφαλὰς</u> Ἄϊδι προϊάψειν,

Iliad XI 55

ii)   In addition the manuscript tradition includes lines 4 and 5, whereas Zeno-dotus (according to schol. A—again Aristonicus) athetized these two lines. This is one of several cases where one of the Alexandrian scholars athetizes a line as well as offering a variant reading for that same line. This indicates clearly that athetesis is not nearly as drastic as outright deletion of a line.

Shipp[56] points out that there is no real parallel involving the opposition of ψυχή 'soul' and αὐτός 'body'; also that ἑλώρια is a *hapax legomenon* in Homer. This would seem to be evidence against ψυχή in line 3, and against lines 4 and 5. However, Apollonius Rhodius (*Argonautica* 2.264) has the only other occur-rence of ἑλώριον, as well as δαῖτα in the previous line, making an apparent allusion to the two lines in Homer. Shipp also notes that *without* lines 4 and 5 either of the two readings in line 3, ψυχάς or κεφαλάς, is satisfactory; *with* these lines only the former is possible, as one cannot contrast head and body. Thus one can explain a change from κεφαλάς to ψυχάς in order to accommo-date lines 4–5, but not a change in the opposite direction.[57]

Bolling[58] is unsure as to whether Zenodotus read ψυχάς or κεφαλάς; but the fact that the scholia stress repeatedly the impossibility of κεφαλάς along with lines 4–5 suggests that it was Z.'s reading. Bolling feels that the shorter text is "superior," giving a better sentence structure: ἐξ οὗ is now closer to μῆνιν ἄειδε, on which it depends (loosely; the former phrase is usually trans-lated 'from the time when'). I draw attention to this statement: "In line 3, when freed from interpolation [i.e. lines 4 and 5], either ψυχάς or κεφαλάς will conform to Homeric usage, so that it is impossible to determine which was the 'original' reading."[59]

---

medieval manuscript Venetus A, written between the primary scholia and the Homeric text. Bolling (1925:43) claims that Aristonicus (whose comments have come to us through the Venetus A scholia) was "waging a relentless war" on Zenodotus, recording even impos-sible variants which he attributed to Z. In this case A. seems to be saying that Zenodotus read κεφαλάς in line 3, as well as including (but athetizing: see Bolling 1944:43) lines 4 and 5; this combination, as mentioned below, does not make good sense.

[56] Shipp 1972:227f.
[57] Shipp also argues that the end of line 5: Διὸς δ' ἐτελείετο βουλή is not "strong" here, and fits better into the *Cypria*; there the earth was weighed down through overpopulation, and so Zeus decided to relieve the pressure by means of the deaths of warriors.
[58] Bolling 1944:43f.
[59] Ibid., 44.

I agree that without lines 4–5, either of the two readings in line 3 is satisfactory; however I would rather say that *both* are acceptable; moreover, the external evidence points also to the authenticity of the version which *includes* lines 4–5 along with the reading ψυχάς in line 3. If we consider these variants from the point of view of oral composition and performance, it seems natural that each reading, given that each has evidence in its favor, can be considered "authentic," and the efforts to determine "originality" become irrelevant.

I give below some of the various possibilities discussed above, with relevant differences highlighted:

a) Μῆνιν ἄειδε θεὰ Πηληϊάδεω Ἀχιλῆος
 οὐλομένην, ἣ μυρί' Ἀχαιοῖς ἄλγε' ἔθηκε,
πολλὰς δ' ἰφθίμους <u>ψυχὰς</u> Ἄϊδι προΐαψεν
ἡρώων, αὐτοὺς δὲ ἑλώρια τεῦχε κύνεσσιν
οἰωνοῖσί τε <u>πᾶσι</u>, Διὸς δ' ἐτελείετο βουλή,   5
ἐξ οὗ δὴ τὰ πρῶτα διαστήτην ἐρίσαντε
Ἀτρεΐδης τε ἄναξ ἀνδρῶν καὶ δῖος Ἀχιλλεύς.

"vulgate"

b) Μῆνιν ἄειδε θεὰ Πηληϊάδεω Ἀχιλῆος
οὐλομένην, ἣ μυρί' Ἀχαιοῖς ἄλγε' ἔθηκε,
πολλὰς δ' ἰφθίμους <u>κεφαλὰς</u> Ἄϊδι προΐαψεν
ἡρώων, αὐτοὺς δὲ ἑλώρια τεῦχε κύνεσσιν
οἰωνοῖσί τε <u>δαῖτα</u>, Διὸς δ' ἐτελείετο βουλή,   5
ἐξ οὗ δὴ τὰ πρῶτα διαστήτην ἐρίσαντε
Ἀτρεΐδης τε ἄναξ ἀνδρῶν καὶ δῖος Ἀχιλλεύς.
"bad" copies, and perhaps Zenodotus according to Aristonicus

c) Μῆνιν ἄειδε θεὰ Πηληϊάδεω Ἀχιλῆος
οὐλομένην, ἣ μυρί' Ἀχαιοῖς ἄλγε' ἔθηκε,
πολλὰς δ' ἰφθίμους <u>ψυχὰς</u> Ἄϊδι προΐαψεν
ἐξ οὗ δὴ τὰ πρῶτα διαστήτην ἐρίσαντε
Ἀτρεΐδης τε ἄναξ ἀνδρῶν καὶ δῖος Ἀχιλλεύς.

"shorter a)"

d) Μῆνιν ἄειδε θεὰ Πηληϊάδεω Ἀχιλῆος
οὐλομένην, ἣ μυρί' Ἀχαιοῖς ἄλγε' ἔθηκε,
πολλὰς δ' ἰφθίμους <u>κεφαλὰς</u> Ἄϊδι προΐαψεν
ἐξ οὗ δὴ τὰ πρῶτα διαστήτην ἐρίσαντε
Ἀτρεΐδης τε ἄναξ ἀνδρῶν καὶ δῖος Ἀχιλλεύς.

"shorter b)"

e) Μῆνιν ἄειδε θεὰ Πηληϊάδεω Ἀχιλῆος
    οὐλομένην, ἣ μυρί' Ἀχαιοῖς ἄλγε' ἔθηκε,
    πολλὰς δ' ἰφθίμους <u>ψυχὰς</u> Ἄϊδι προΐαψεν
    ἡρώων, αὐτοὺς δὲ ἑλώρια τεῦχε κύνεσσιν
    οἰωνοῖσί τε <u>δαῖτα</u>, Διὸς δ' ἐτελείετο βουλή,   5
    ἐξ οὗ δὴ τὰ πρῶτα διαστήτην ἐρίσαντε
    Ἀτρεΐδης τε ἄναξ ἀνδρῶν καὶ δῖος Ἀχιλλεύς.
    Zenodotus, but including lines 4 and 5

f) Μῆνιν ἄειδε θεὰ Πηληϊάδεω Ἀχιλῆος
    οὐλομένην, ἣ μυρί' Ἀχαιοῖς ἄλγε' ἔθηκε,
    πολλὰς δ' ἰφθίμους <u>κεφαλὰς</u> Ἄϊδι προΐαψεν
    ἡρώων, αὐτοὺς δὲ ἑλώρια τεῦχε κύνεσσιν
    οἰωνοῖσί τε <u>πᾶσι</u>, Διὸς δ' ἐτελείετο βουλή,   5
    ἐξ οὗ δὴ τὰ πρῶτα διαστήτην ἐρίσαντε
    Ἀτρεΐδης τε ἄναξ ἀνδρῶν καὶ δῖος Ἀχιλλεύς.
    another possibility . . .

By seeing each of these six "variants" simultaneously, the reader can make his or her own decision as to preference,[60] and also get a sense of some of the history of the transmission of the text over time. Such is rather more difficult to do with the traditional layout, with the "main" text at the top of the page, and the variants, usually in fragmented form, in the *apparatus criticus* at the bottom.[61]

I have cited this passage and these scholars' opinions concerning the variants at some length, in order to show once again how prevalent are the assumptions behind judgments about the correctness or otherwise of variant readings in Homer. I next consider conventional views concerning the fixation and subsequent transmission of the Homeric text, and offer my own suggestions in the light of my understanding of oral composition, performance, and transmission.

Current views on the transmission of the Homeric text generally include the assumption that an archetype of some sort was written some time be-

[60] See A. di Luzio, below, p. 58.
[61] West's new Teubner edition of the *Iliad* (West 1998 and 2000) follows this traditional format, although he does include a vast number of variant readings, including Alexandrian conjectures and "eccentric" papyrus variants. In a later work (West 2001:158) he states that his aim is "the best approximation that may be possible to the *Iliad* as its original author left it." Nagy, on the other hand (2004:69), argues that "the evidence of textual multiformity precludes a uniform reconstruction, a 'unitext' edition of Homer." I hope to offer support for Nagy's position later in this present work.

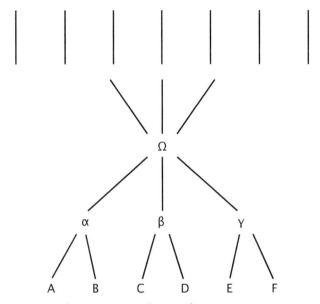

Figure 2. The conventional view of Homeric transmission.

tween the eighth and sixth centuries BCE, perhaps by means of dictation by an ἀοιδός, and that all our extant papyrus and manuscript copies derive from this archetype.[62] These views generally must assume that the practices of oral performance and "re-creation" either died out around the time this archetype was written down,[63] or that such practices continued but were irrelevant to the subsequent history of the written Homeric text, i.e. that they had no perceptible effect on it. Along these lines Janko has proposed 750–725 BCE and 743–713 BCE for the dates (of the final written form) of the *Iliad* and *Odyssey* respectively, based on his counts of certain linguistic criteria, as well as comparisons with Hesiod and the *Homeric Hymns*.[64]

Figure 2 above illustrates this conventional view of Homeric textual transmission: the top row of vertical lines represents fluid oral transmission

---

[62] E.g. Bolling 1925:41; Jensen 1980:11.

[63] Nagy 1996a:152: "It is unnecessary, however, for proponents of an 'oral Homer' to insist on one and only one right version, unless they are also willing to believe that the oral tradition ground to a dead halt sometime around the second half of the eighth century BCE, after the text was supposedly dictated."

[64] Janko 1982:228–231. Apart from his assumption of the static nature of the text, Janko's methodology assumes a steady rate of change in these criteria; he admits this is potentially problematic but sees no reason to abandon it. One needs to be cautious in this regard, particularly in view of the problems inherent in the once-popular concept of "glottochronology," which assumed a constant rate of attrition in the core vocabulary of a language.

up until the eighth (Janko), seventh (M. West[65]), or sixth (Jensen[66]) century BCE. At this point oral transmission fades or ceases altogether, but first an archetype (Ω) is written down, by means of dictation or otherwise.[67] From here on the Homeric text behaves exactly like a written text, and we can imagine a stemma which theoretically explains all surviving manuscripts, inasmuch as they are descended from this archetype. This archetype is equivalent to Bolling's "fountainhead";[68] Greek letters stand for non-extant and Roman letters for extant manuscripts, as in "regular" stemmata. Even to think of Homeric transmission in these terms—as most scholars apparently do, at least subconsciously—necessarily leads one to want to find an archetype for the Homeric text, as well as to feel constrained to choose between "genuine" and "spurious" readings whenever the need arises.

Needless to say, I believe that the conventional model is illogical. There is evidence that Homeric performance traditions continued into Ptolemaic times,[69] and indeed did affect the written Homeric texts, some small portion of which we possess today. Nagy adduces iconographical evidence which supports his theory of an evolutionary process of textualization. In particular he discusses sixth-century vases which show versions of Iliadic themes that vary from our *Iliad*,[70] and also mentions non-Homeric verse inscriptions which act not as transcripts of a performance but as equivalent to the performance itself;[71] such evidence points to the extreme unlikelihood of there having been a fixed written text before this time. He suggests that such text-fixation cannot have happened until the time when such variations have faded: around 530 B.C. may be a possible *terminus post quem* for the textualization or quasi-textualization of the *Iliad* and *Odyssey*.[72] However this date does not indi-

---

[65] West 1990.

[66] Jensen 1980.

[67] Those scholars, such as Jensen, who accept the theory of the "Pisistratean Recension" see it as playing a fundamental role in the fixing of the final form of the text. I note that when she says (Jensen 1980:9) that "the *Iliad* and the *Odyssey* were orally composed, and . . . their composition took place in the sixth century BCE on the initiative of Pisistratus," she appears by the term "composition" to mean "putting into written form," a confusing use of terminology. On the question of the "Pisistratean Recension," I agree with Boyd, who convincingly argues against its historicity, concluding (1995:45) that it represents an attempt by "earlier literate people (e.g. Cicero) to create an image which would capture for them the concept of a Homer before their own time."

[68] Bolling 1925:41.

[69] Nagy (1996a:144–145) claims that performance traditions of Homer persisted for several centuries after 150 BCE.

[70] Nagy 1996b:106ff. Also see n19 above.

[71] Ibid., 35f.

[72] Ibid., 108.

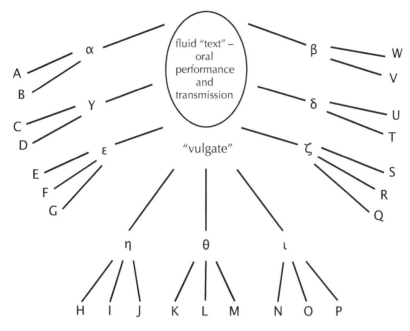

Figure 3. An alternative view of Homeric transmission.

cate a sudden fixing of the text, but rather the transcribing or recording of performances; such transcriptions would in no way have *replaced* live performances.[73]

Figure 3 illustrates a scheme which takes into account the continuation of oral performance traditions (time moves from top to bottom): we have a period of fluid transmission lasting well into the Ptolemaic period and beyond. During this long period, Homer's poetry is performed, and texts in the sense of "transcripts" are written down.[74] These non-extant (or possibly extant) transcripts are represented by Greek letters; from them our "eccentric" manuscripts, such as the Ptolemaic papyri (represented by letters A–G and Q–W), will have been copied. Those classical authors who quote lines of Homer may well not have depended on written texts at all; their versions of Homer will have derived from one or other of the various and varied performance traditions with which they will have been familiar. There may therefore be no obvious or necessary

---

[73] Ibid., 100f. Nagy also disagrees with Merkelbach's view that repeated performances by rhapsodes would have led to the disintegration of the text without the primacy of a written manuscript—the concept of "zersingen."

[74] For a definition of this term see Nagy 1996a:112.

distinction between the "eccentric" text of a Ptolemaic papyrus and the divergent text of a Homeric quotation in Plato or Aeschines[75]: both will derive, at
not too many steps removed, from a "current" performance.

Towards the end of this period of textual fluidity, at around 150 BCE,
the standard text or "vulgate" comes into existence, and the majority of our
medieval manuscripts (letters H–P) reflect this "textus receptus." Now if we
consider the dates of our "best" medieval manuscripts, such as Venetus A, we
see that they were written centuries later than the date of the performances
from which they derive. On the other hand, such texts as the Ptolemaic papyri,
inasmuch as they were written while performance traditions were still "alive,"
represent texts very close in time to their "originals." And yet we shall see
that even medieval manuscripts like Venetus A can preserve ancient readings
which provide evidence of much earlier performance traditions.

Because we can never identify a single unique "original" version of
Homer's epic, and because new "authentic" versions were being created
and recreated in performance throughout the period of oral transmission, it
follows that any written records that survive from this period when oral transmission was alive and well are in all likelihood records (whether firsthand or
a few times removed) of these authentic versions, and hence should be given
the weight due to documents that are close in time to their "original source,"
i.e. the Homeric performance from which they derive.

I compare this situation with that of modern (and a few ancient) authors
who have made alterations to their own works, either before or after publication, with the result that more than one "authentic" version gets into circulation. Examples include Matteo Maria Boiardo's *Amorum libri*[76] and William
Wordsworth's *The Prelude*.[77] This situation has been handled by printing the
multiple versions in parallel, a procedure which allows the reader to compare
versions and trace developments in the author's thought and style over time.
This is what the Homer Multitext project aims to do in the case of the *Iliad* and
the *Odyssey*.

If indeed our documentary evidence is so close to its "original" performances, then it may be more appropriate to treat it in the way that more
modern editors treat their texts. Tarrant discusses the differences in approach
between classical and modern editors, describing how in the case of the former,
the original text, inasmuch as it is felt to be distant from its editors, both in
time and in generations of copies, tends to gain a sort of idealized perfection,

---

[75] See Dué 2001.
[76] See Cherchi 1995:448.
[77] See Reiman 1995:311f.

and correspondingly the manuscripts themselves are liable to be depreciated.[78] For the modern editor, on the other hand, because the documents are felt to be so much closer to the original work, their importance is magnified: indeed different authorial versions as well as versions produced by copyists are given high regard, and we find statements such as: "a work encompasses all its authorial versions and . . . all of them should be read in order to experience a work fully."[79] I suggest that at least some of our texts of Homer deserve to be treated in precisely this same way—that they are in effect "versions" of Homeric poetry, and all deserve to be read in order for the scholar to experience Homer fully. The difference, of course, is that instead of assuming the existence of a single author called "Homer,"[80] we are viewing each ἀοιδός as an authentic composer/performer of Homer's poetry.[81]

While on the topic of "authorial versions," I refer again to Martin West's treatise on textual criticism.[82] In his discussion of the ways in which textual variation arises in a text, he states that the first such way "is that the author himself may change it, after copies have already gone into circulation."[83] Examples given include Aristophanes, Apollonius Rhodius, and Ovid. West states that this type of variation can be evidenced by "major divergences between different branches of the tradition, if both versions convince the connoisseur of their authenticity."[84] Further on, West gives guidelines for determining if there is unlikely to have been a single archetype: firstly, "from the presence in the medieval tradition of many pairs of variants known to be ancient," and secondly, "from the presence of divergences so substantial . . . or so early . . . that one cannot believe them to have arisen in the short time available or under the conditions that prevailed after the end of antiquity."[85] In other words, in the kinds of texts envisaged by West, it is extremely unlikely either that one variant arose from the other by some form of corruption, or

---

[78] Tarrant 1995:96–98.

[79] Tanselle 1995:26.

[80] I note for comparison the Provençal *troubadour* Jaufré Rudel: in editing his texts, Pickens (1978:40) concluded that "the conventions and traditions of the courtly lyric have conspired to efface the author and to create at least as many Jaufré Rudels as there are medieval anthologies" (quoted in Nagy 1996a:12).

[81] I also mention here Tarrant 1989 ("Collaborative Interpolation"); although Tarrant is writing about written Latin literature, the principle of collaboration between author and reader—or, *mutatis mutandis*, singer and hearer—is, I think, potentially fruitful for our understanding of the transmission of Homeric epic poetry.

[82] West 1973.

[83] Ibid., 15.

[84] Ibid., 16.

[85] Ibid., 41–42.

that the two variants share a common origin, with both being derived from a third, original reading. West also states that the aim should be "to determine which of the manuscripts or manuscript families are most independent of each other, for these must go back most directly to the earliest phases of the tradition that we can reach, and they must be the most fruitful sources of ancient readings."[86]

It seems to me that when West's criteria are used, a large number of sets of variant readings preserved in the Homeric manuscripts and other sources do indeed point to there being no single archetype for the Homeric text. We have already seen at the beginning of the *Iliad* a pair of variants, both "known to be ancient," and we will see many more examples of "major divergences" that are both substantial and ancient; in addition it is clear that many of the sources of these sets of variants are independent of each other. I cite T. W. Allen's attempts to create families of Homeric manuscripts, as part of his effort to trace back the lines of textual transmission. In his endeavors to discover the history of the Homeric text, he is unable to construct a single stemma, and instead creates twenty-four textual families or "sub-stemmata," by comparing variant readings shared by various uncials, minuscules, and papyri.[87] And even these attempts are deemed unsuccessful (except for *one* of Allen's families—h) by later scholars.[88]

Further on in his book, West lists the requirements that the "correct" reading must fulfill (assuming there is one "correct" reading). I draw attention to his third requirement:

> It must be fully compatible with the fact that the surviving sources give what they do; in other words it must be clear how the presumed original reading could have been corrupted into any different reading that is transmitted.[89]

On the next page he points out that *plausibility* is no guarantee of genuineness, since there is a multitude of places (in classical literature) where more than one of the surviving variants is plausible.[90] Indeed, apart from the minority of cases where a scribe appears to have copied something unintelligible (to him

---

[86] Ibid., 43.
[87] Allen 1931.I. The "sub-stemmata" are in chart form, following p. 278.
[88] Janko 1992:20n3; Pasquali 1952:208. Haslam (1997:89–90nn99, 103) notes that some of the criticism of Allen has been "vicious" and rallies to his defense, pointing out some of the ways in which Allen has been misunderstood and worse.
[89] West 1973:48.
[90] Ibid., 49.

as well as to us),[91] I suspect most variants survive precisely because they are plausible.[92]

Of course the problem with so many Homeric variants is precisely that: it is *impossible* the see how "the presumed original reading could have been corrupted" into one or more of the other variants. To quote Stephanie West once again, variants in the Ptolemaic papyri "tend to differ markedly from the traditional text in a way which cannot be explained by the processes of merely mechanical corruption."[93] And although a few pages later she concludes that there is no clear connection between the extent of interpolations in these papyri and the "long oral tradition of the poems,"[94] in a later work she says that even the papyri dated after 150 BCE "offer too wide a range of variants to allow the hypothesis that they might all be copies of a single edition."[95] This is after claiming that a presumed sixth-century recension "must be regarded as the archetype of all our Homeric manuscripts and of the indirect tradition represented by ancient quotations and allusions."[96]

For a similar example of seeming ambivalence between the single archetype hypothesis and a willingness to consider the effects of oral transmission, I cite Richard Janko's statement:

> All our manuscripts somehow go back to a single origin, and have passed through a single channel; it is improbable that more than one "original" of the *Iliad* ever existed, even if different rhapsodic performances and editorial interventions have led to the addition or (rarely) omission of verses here and there. This basic fixity needs to be explained.[97]

I contrast this statement with his earlier remarks about the extent of textual variation in the text of Homer and the *Homeric Hymns*, as evidenced by a quotation in Thucydides:

> [The quotation by Thucydides, III 104] presents a number of variants that amount to much more than straightforward corruptions or fail-

---

[91] See e.g. the example from Plutarch in the previous chapter, pp. 8–9.
[92] Compare Wolf's observation that often the most "offensive" readings turn out to be genuine, while those most plausible and witty must be rejected as being of no authority: Wolf 1985:59–61.
[93] S. West 1967:11.
[94] Ibid., 13.
[95] S. West 1988:47.
[96] Ibid., 39.
[97] Janko 1992:29.

ures of memory . . . these variants are just what we might expect to find in a recasting of the song by an oral singer or reciter.[98]

Further on,

These fluctuations strongly suggest oral transmission and recomposition . . . versions of what is essentially the same poem could undergo substantial change, apparently by oral transmission involving some recomposition: these versions appear to be different recordings of the same underlying *Gestalt*.[99]

But then he is constrained to make a choice between these variants, and we find, for example, where the two versions of the *Hymn to Hermes* (*Hy 4* and *Hy 18*) present different readings, "thus *Hy 4* is *better* here."[100]

Mention of the two versions of the *Homeric Hymn to Hermes* brings me to another important concept—that of expansion and contraction (or compression). *Hymn 4* with 580 lines stands in significant contrast to *Hymn 18*, which has only 12 lines. Nagy, in discussing the long and short versions of the *Homeric Hymn to Hermes*, notes that the expansion and compression involved in such differing treatments is a clear indication of oral poetics.[101] I refer also to the words of Parry quoted at the beginning of this chapter, where he describes how a singer sings: "he will leave out and add whole passages as the time and the mood of his hearers calls for a fuller or a briefer telling of a tale or of a given part of a tale."[102] Lord too, throughout his work, stresses the ability of the singer to "lengthen or shorten a song according to his own desires and to create a new song if he sees fit."[103] At the end of one chapter he lists six ways in which the singer can change his story: these include having fewer or more lines, "expansion of ornamentation," and addition or omission of material.[104]

I see this principle of contraction and expansion applying on two related levels. First, we will see shortly examples of type-scenes within the *Iliad* and *Odyssey* that are widely used and that can be changed in length as the context demands. The poet can tell of a sacrifice or an arming in more than way and

---

[98] Janko 1982:2.

[99] Ibid., 3.

[100] Ibid.; my emphasis.

[101] Nagy 1990:55. The longer *Hymn* contains a lengthy narrative which is not included in the shorter *Hymn*, but which Nagy argues can be viewed as an example of expansion. He also compares the case of *Hymn 25* and Hesiod's *Theogony*.

[102] Parry 1971:336, cited in n12 above.

[103] Lord 1960:26. Cf. Nagy 1996b:77: "We should expect to find in living oral traditions . . . [that] the context of a given occasion leads to shortening or lengthening by default."

[104] Lord 1960:123.

at greater or lesser length, depending on poetic context. Second, as the Homeric poems were performed and transmitted orally over time, shorter and longer versions must have been heard and eventually written down, leaving us with texts that appear to have "plus verses" and also those with "minus verses." However, scholars such as Bolling and Apthorp, looking at shorter and longer versions of passages of Homer, choose to see only expansion, never contraction, leading them to generally label all lines that are in one text and not another as interpolations.[105] While this may be applicable for works that were never transmitted orally, it is an unwarranted assumption in the case of Homer. Even when Apthorp says that he is allowing for the operation of oral transmission, for him this seems to mean merely that a fixed number of lines, which everyone knew, was sung by singers and passed on to other singers, with the occasional lapse of memory causing a line or two to be left out from time to time.[106] This is hardly the way true oral transmission takes place.

It is true that over time the story as told by poets expands overall, with the *Iliad* and *Odyssey* being, as Nagy says, the "ultimate expansion." Indeed this monumental expansion makes it difficult to appreciate the phenomenon of compression, but it is there nevertheless, and we should not constrain ourselves into seeing either the expanded or the compressed version as "basic."[107]

At this point I return to the text of Homer and look at further examples of passages where, to use Martin West's words, there are "major divergences between different branches of the tradition, [and] both versions convince the connoisseur of their authenticity."[108] These examples will also serve as illustrations of compression and expansion.[109]

Since Zenodotus is the earliest of the three great Alexandrian scholars, I consider first another example involving his readings.[110] He has the reputation of being the most "conservative" of the three (in the sense of having the

---

[105] I further discuss Bolling and Apthorp below, pp. 55–58.

[106] Apthorp 1980:xv.

[107] Nagy 1996b:76–77.

[108] West 1973:16.

[109] Nagy (2004:61–62) sees so-called "interpolations" as potential cases of expansion and compression (he use the term "vertical variants"), and *variae lectiones* as cases of "intralinear formulaic variation" ("horizontal variants").

[110] I realize that our knowledge of Zenodotus' readings derives from the later scholia, and that the possibility is always present that such scholia may be presenting their own views rather than those of Zenodotus. As noted above in n55, Bolling (1925:43) thinks that the scholia which go back to Aristonicus are polemical against Zenodotus, frequently quoting supposed readings of Z. in order to make him look foolish. For an example of Aristonicus carefully recording an "impossible" reading of Zenodotus, see *Iliad* I 446f.

shortest text; those who consider him as a "hacker of the text" would see him as the *least* conservative). His "alterations" to the text can be the most minor details (e.g. νῶϊν for νῷϊ at *Iliad* VIII 377); they include variations in one word (e.g. δαῖτα for πᾶσι at *Iliad* I 5[111]); and extend even to the rejection of whole groups of lines (e.g. *Iliad* I 396-406). One of the more significant ways in which Zenodotus' readings differ from those of the "vulgate" is in his treatment of groups of lines. Sometimes he appears to contract two lines into one, e.g. *Iliad* I 219f., 446f., etc.; in *Iliad* II 55 he expands one line into two; in *Iliad* II 60-70 he contracts eleven lines into two; and so on.[112] In cases where there is no extant manuscript support for his readings, scholars have often assumed that he was indulging in pure conjecture.[113] In cases where there is some support, one might suppose that it was Zenodotus' reading which has given rise to the (later) manuscript evidence. There are a few cases, however, where the only support for a Zenodotean reading is to be found in a relatively early papyrus, thus raising the possibility that Zenodotus had available to him a text with the given reading already in it, in other words, reversing the direction of the influence.

In *Iliad* IV 88f., where the "vulgate" has the two lines:

Πάνδαρον ἀντίθεον διζημένη, εἴ που ἐφεύροι
εὗρε Λυκάονος υἱὸν ἀμύμονά τε κρατερόν τε

Looking for godlike Pandarus, if somehow she (Athena) might find him;
She found the blameless and strong son of Lycaon.

Zenodotus[114] has the single line:

Πάνδαρον ἀντίθεον διζημένη, εὗρε δὲ τόνδε.

Looking for godlike Pandarus, and she found him.

This variant is found in no extant manuscript, except for the Ptolemaic papyrus P41. P41, which contains portions of books III, IV and V of the *Iliad*, is dated by Allen to the third century BCE,[115] and more specifically by S. West

---

[111] See above, pp. 34–37.

[112] Other examples from the first four books of the *Iliad*: II 156–168 contracted to one line; II 681 and 718 "altered"; III 423–426 contracted into one line; in IV 123f. the order of lines is reversed. In all of these example, the evidence is from the scholia to Venetus A, and once from Eustathius. See West 2001:41 for a complete list of Zenodotean "abridgements."

[113] E.g., van der Valk passim.

[114] Scholia to these lines in the manuscript Venetus A.

[115] Allen 1931.I:6.

to 280–240 BCE.[116] West considers the possibility that the papyrus reading is due to the influence of Zenodotus' text, but thinks it more likely that the debt was the other way around: "On the other hand, Zenodotus must have had MS. support for some, if not for all, of his readings."[117]

Both readings are clearly "acceptable" in terms of grammar and flow of thought; the "vulgate" includes epithets complimentary to Pandarus, which Zenodotus (and thus presumably his source) omits. The variation in each version could easily be explained as a difference in emphasis, arising from different versions. As well as calling Pandarus αἰσχροκερδής ('sordidly greedy of gain', *LSJ*) and ἡ πάντων ἀρά ('the curse of all'), the scholia discuss how the longer version appears to be overly "anthropomorphic": why would the goddess Athena need to look around for Pandarus, as if she didn't know where he was? In line with Zenodotus' supposed concept of τὸ πρέπον ('what is appropriate'), Leaf says that "Zenodotus was offended at the doubt which he thought was expressed as to the certainty of the goddess finding him [Pandarus]."[118] On the other hand, the other point of view is also mentioned in the scholia, namely that when a god or goddess takes human form, he or she has to resort to human activities.[119] Thus each reading can be supported by both internal and external evidence. To repeat, both the short and the long version have ancient support, and both can be justified on the grounds of language and narrative flow. Rengakos notes that Apollonius Rhodius in *Argonautica* 3.113f. conflates the "vulgate" and the Zenodotean text, proving that Zenodotus' reading, far from being a conjecture, must have depended on documentary material.[120]

I mention for comparison a line from book xii of the *Odyssey*. To put the line into context: Odysseus and his men have anchored their ship on the island of the sun god; whilst Odysseus is elsewhere on the island, his men, desperate for food, have decided, against the orders of Odysseus, that it would be better to kill and eat the cattle of the sun god and risk sudden destruction, than to starve to death slowly. So, after rounding up the cattle, they prepare to sacrifice them. Usually such a sacrifice would include the sprinkling of white barley; but as none was available, oak leaves had to suffice. Thus we get the following line:

---

[116] S. West 1967:64.

[117] Ibid., 69.

[118] Leaf 1902:160.

[119] Scholia in manuscripts A and T; also the D-scholia.

[120] Rengakos 1993:58f. He also compares the identical passage *Iliad* V 168f., where because the subject is human (as opposed to divine in IV 88f.), no variant readings have been recorded.

αὐτὰρ ἐπεί ῥ' εὔξαντο καὶ ἔσφαξαν καὶ ἔδειραν,

But when they had prayed and cut the throats (of the cattle) and
flayed them . . .

Odyssey xii 359

The more "usual" sacrifice formulation has *two* lines, which include the sprinkling of the barley, as well as the drawing back of the victims' heads:

<u>αὐτὰρ ἐπεί ῥ' εὔξαντο</u> καὶ οὐλοχύτας προβάλοντο,
αὐέρυσαν μὲν πρῶτα <u>καὶ ἔσφαξαν καὶ ἔδειραν</u>,

<u>But when they had prayed</u> and sprinkled the barley-grains,
they first drew back (the victims' heads) <u>and cut their throats and
flayed them</u> . . .

Iliad I 458–459; also II 421–422

I highlight the pieces of the two lines from the "expanded" version which have
been used for the "shorter" version. In the *Odyssey* passage, the lack of barley
grains leads to the omission of the second half of the first line, and thus also the
pulling back of the victims' heads in the first half of the second line. In other
words, we have here an "abbreviated" version of part of the regular sacrificial
form, based on differences in the narrative context. Thus we note the existence of a "long" and a "short" version of a particular element in a type-scene,
each tailored to fit into its respective context. So when we find evidence for
both a "long" and a "short" version belonging to the *same* passage, we must at
least allow for the possibility that both are valid and "original."

In looking at other examples of "typical scenes," in particular of sacri-
fices, I notice that there is considerable flexibility in retaining or omitting
"essential" elements. For instance, in the two sacrifice episodes of *Iliad* I and
II (I 458–469 and II 421–432), ten of the twelve lines are identical, and in the
same order. However when we move to *Odyssey* iii (447–473), we get only five
of these same lines, and in a much longer passage overall. By way of contrast,
in *Odyssey* xii (359–365) we find a considerably shorter version, but still with
six of these lines. In each of the *Odyssey* passages a flexibility of composition is
exhibited which should lead us to treat with a more open mind passages, like
that discussed above, where more than one version of an episode is preserved.
I note too that Edwards, in a useful article summarizing scholarship on the
subject of "typical scenes," points out that "use of type-scenes is probably
a better test for orality, at least in Greek poetry, than use of formulae."[121] He

---

[121] Edwards 1992:289. Edwards observes that Parry had already noted this in 1933–35: Parry
1971:451–452.

also indicates that more work needs to be done on how type-scene structure relates to oral versus written style.[122]

The passage from *Iliad* IV brings up the subject of interpolation: one of the characteristic features of the Ptolemaic papyri (to be discussed in the next chapter) is that they often possess "plus verses," and many if not most scholars generally judge these to be both "spurious" and "inferior." During the twentieth and early twenty-first centuries two scholars in particular, Bolling and Apthorp, have devoted themselves to the question of interpolation in Homer. In three books published in 1925,[123] 1944, [124]and 1950, G. M. Bolling sought to rid our text of Homer of all "spurious" lines, and his studies culminated with his edition of the "Athenian Homer"—the so-called Π-text, containing about 14,650 lines, reflecting the *Iliad* that he believed must have been current in sixth-century Athens.[125] Between the sixth and second centuries, approximately one thousand "extraneous" lines were added to this text, with the result that Aristarchus' text—which Bolling calls the "Alpha text"—contains about 15,600 lines.[126] Each of these "interpolated" lines was in Aristarchus' text, but many were marked with the obelus, indicating that Aristarchus considered the external evidence for them to be too weak to establish their authenticity.[127] In many cases, however (e.g. *Iliad* I 4–5, II 60–70, etc.), Aristarchus judged as genuine lines which Zenodotus had athetised. Bolling generally excludes these lines as well, looking for the "lowest common denominator" in order to establish his sixth-century "archetype"; thus if he finds two manuscripts covering the same passage, but which do not both include the same number of lines, i.e. one omits some lines while the other omits different lines, Bolling will only judge as belonging to his Π-text those lines which are in both manuscripts.[128] There are also a few cases where Bolling leaves in the text lines which Aristarchus had athetised (in book I lines 29–30 and line 96).

---

[122] Edwards 1992:290. On type-scenes see also Arend 1933, reviewed by Milman Parry in Parry 1971:404–407, first published in 1936; Lord 1960:68–98 and 186–197; Fenik 1968; and Kirk 1962, 1985, and 1990.

[123] Bolling 1925.

[124] Bolling 1944.

[125] Bolling 1950. I note that Bolling (1925:34) states that Wolf "did conceive the margins of the Pisistratean edition as filled with variants." While I would agree with Bolling that no such written *apparatus criticus* existed at that time, yet I believe that such variants were indeed in existence, being circulated and transmitted orally. Bolling's rigid views on the state of the Homeric text, even at this early date, preclude any such possibility.

[126] Bolling 1950:4.

[127] See Bird 2009, where I discuss in detail the ways in which "critical signs" (including the obelus) are used in the Venetus A manuscript of the *Iliad*.

[128] See Bolling 1950:7 for an example from *Iliad* XII 175–195, and see Bolling's resultant Π-text ad loc. On p. 8 he says, "Every text had the lines of Π for its core . . ."

Bolling's language throughout indicates that he is conceiving of a purely written transmission; in addition he frequently stresses his assumption that texts always expand and never contract.

> Mechanical blunders barred, each of our manuscripts contains the text of Aristarchus together with more or less extraneous material.

Also,

> In the same way, each of the pre-Aristarchean mss. contained the text of Pisistratus, together with the addition of a greater or less number of other verses.

And

> Every line of the genuine text was contained in every edition.[129]

Bolling also approvingly gives this quotation from Leaf:

> "[there is] no single case in Homer where the loss of a line can be assumed . . . the tradition was wonderfully tenacious of all it had got as well as acquisitive of new matter."

Bolling rescues Zenodotus from the charge of "hacking at the text," made by scholars who have assumed that the longer text is original, and states that

> interpolation is a well-established fact, but the proof of hacking is still to seek.[130]

Two further quotations illustrate clearly how completely bound Bolling is to the concept of a written archetype, with no allowance for the mechanics of oral performance and transmission:

> Whenever there are known to have existed longer and shorter versions of a passage the difference between them must be due to interpolation.[131]

And

> I shall, of course, be compelled to examine also those passages in which there seems to be, but is not, evidence for the existence of two versions.[132]

[129] Bolling 1925:42–43.
[130] Ibid., 53.
[131] Ibid., 55.
[132] Ibid., 56.

In fairness one should note that these statements were published in 1925, before the appearance of Parry's seminal work; however, Bolling in 1950 (well after Parry's death) could still write:

> When a passage is known to have stood in one text and to have been absent from another . . . the difference . . . has been brought about by expansion, not by contraction of the text.[133]

The second of the two scholars, M. Apthorp, has continued the work of Bolling, using recent papyrus discoveries to reinforce Bolling's arguments, and sometimes re-stating points which he feels Bolling did not make forcefully enough.[134] Apthorp gives some credence to oral performance and transmission, and yet he appears to misunderstand how it would work: "even when due allowance has been made for the operation of oral transmission (and thus omission through a reciter's forgetfulness), in conjunction with the written transmission, . . . the lines omitted by Aristarchus were spurious."[135] In other words oral transmission means little more than singers simply memorizing and "reciting" songs; in the course of reciting a song some lines may be left out due to forgetfulness and hence get left out of one or more manuscripts.

Apthorp does explicitly allow that Parry's theory of oral transmission and the way it can explain divergences in the written transmission "remains plausible";[136] and yet imagining that the chief way for a line to be omitted is through "a reciter's forgetfulness" shows that he too is thinking in terms of an archetype, ultimately written. His use of terms such as "spurious" leads him, as it did Bolling, to reject all those "additional lines" which occur in the Ptolemaic papyri, in the scholia, and in the quotations, because of their weak attestation in surviving manuscripts, and because (in most cases) Aristarchus does not seem to know of them.[137] This use of Aristarchus as the sole "filter" through whom alone all "genuine" lines had to pass seems to be a problem with the approach of Bolling and Apthorp.[138] There seems to be no good reason why "genuine" lines could not have "got around" him and made it into the later

---

[133] Bolling 1950:11–12. Apthorp (1980:xxi) notes that even after the appearance of Parry's work Bolling repeated his previous arguments with "no concessions to Parry."

[134] Apthorp 1980. On p. xx Apthorp indicates that Bolling sometimes underplayed the strength of his own arguments.

[135] Ibid., xv.

[136] Ibid., xxii.

[137] Ibid., xvi.

[138] Apthorp (1980:xvi) describes his task as preventing spurious or interpolated lines from "reaching the Eden of authenticity," by which he means presumably that paradise consists solely of genuine lines allowed in by Aristarchus.

manuscript tradition without ever coming to his attention.[139] And we should never rule out the possibility that Aristarchus "made mistakes"—a possibility both Bolling and Apthorp seem very reluctant to admit.

In seeking to show that various variant readings and "plus verses" are in fact authentic, one may use the tools of comparative philology and formulaic analysis.[140] Nagy uses the former to show that certain readings are ancient and thus authentic (but not "superior").[141] In addition, such evidence can be used to show that oral performance traditions continued far later than is generally accepted. I refer to some cases where even seemingly "insignificant" variants can provide important evidence about the transmission of the Homeric text. Following a conjecture by Wackernagel, Nagy adduces the following sets of variants. Of each pair of variants, the first is transmitted in the majority of manuscripts, but its accent is "anomalous"; the second has the "regular" accent and is reported as a variant. In each case the word with the anomalous accent can be shown by comparative Indo-European linguistics to be archaic.[142]

θαμειαί	θαμεῖαι		'thick'	(*Iliad* I 52)
καυστειρῆς	καυστείρης (also καυστηρῆς)		'blazing'	(*Iliad* IV 342)
ταρφειαί	ταρφεῖαι		'thick'	(*Iliad* XIX 357)
ἀγυιῇ	ἀγυίῃ[143]		'street'	(*Odyssey* xv 441)

Nagy argues that this kind of accentual variation was "not derived by the Alexandrian exegetes from spoken dialectal pronunciation, but rather, from intense research in recited rhapsodic pronunciation."[144] Since accents do not appear to have been considered to be an integral part of the written text by Aristarchus and other Alexandrians, the variants given above suggest that such information about them could not have depended solely upon written exemplars—rather there was another kind of evidence available, namely

---

[139] Conversely, I note Stephanie West's comment (1967:13) that: "It is disconcerting to have to admit the possibility that authentic lines may have been lost after surviving until the second century BC."

[140] Nagy 1996a:133. I point out that Nagy uses these criteria to test authenticity, not correctness.

[141] Ibid., 148. He makes reference there to evidence from Linear B.

[142] Ibid., 128ff.; also Nagy 1970:120–122.

[143] As an illustration of how editors of Homer have very different ideas of what constitutes a "significant" variant, I compare the *Odyssey* editions of von der Muehll and van Thiel. Von der Muehll's edition, although its apparatus criticus is much less detailed, nevertheless lists this variant; van Thiel's, on the other hand, with its much fuller apparatus, sees fit to ignore it. See also West 2001:161. West himself does cite these variants in his Teubner edition.

[144] Nagy 1970:121. He also cites passages from Wackernagel and Lehrs which suggest that they were thinking along similar lines.

the evidence of performance traditions, which were thus still current at that time.

Another example of an ancient form being preserved by scholia and also in one or more medieval manuscripts involves the pair of variants τ' ἄρ and ταρ. In most modern editions the beginnings of these three lines from the first book of the *Iliad* are printed as follows:

1.8:   τίς τ' ἄρ . . .
1.65: εἴτ' ἄρ' . . .
1.93: οὔ τ' ἄρ . . .   (or οὔτ' ἄρ)

The German linguist Wackernagel had proposed the readings:

1.8:   τίς ταρ
1.65: εἴ ταρ
1.93: οὔ ταρ

The first two of these readings occur in the manuscript Venetus A (in 93 Ven. A has the unusual οὔτὰρ), and are explicitly commented upon there by the scholiast—generally thought to derive from Herodian. Subsequently comparative evidence—from the Luvian language (Luvian kuiš=tar is equivalent to Homeric τίς ταρ), which was unknown to Wackernagel—has come to light which provides strong support for the antiquity of the reading ταρ.[145] Thus we have yet more evidence for the survival of ancient forms in later manuscripts,[146] and more evidence that oral performance traditions continued for a lot longer than is commonly believed.

As an illustration of how the technique of formulaic analysis can be used to demonstrate the authenticity of more than one variant in a given passage, I cite *Iliad* VIII 526, in which the following three variants are reported by various papyri:

a)   εὔχομαι ἐλπόμενος Διί τ' ἄλλοισίν τε θεοῖσιν

   I pray in hope to Zeus and the other gods . . .
                                    "vulgate," T. W. Allen's OCT

   External evidence: most mss.; a scholion in Venetus A—Erbse's A[im]—the authority is stated to be "οὕτως ἡ γραφή"—which appears to mean Aristarchus; also P486a—a third-century CE papyrus.

---

[145] Watkins 1995:150–151.
[146] I note Nagy's statement (1996a:148): "In general, a most convincing proof of a variant's authenticity is its relative archaism."

b) ἔλπομαι εὐχόμενος Διί τ' ἄλλοισίν τε θεοῖσιν[147]
    I hope, praying to Zeus and the other gods . . .
    Zenodotus, T. W. Allen's *editio maior*[148]

    External evidence: some other mss.; another scholion in Venetus A;
    Plutarch *Vita Homeri* ii 118.

c) εὔχομαι δ' ἐλπόμενος Διί τ' ἄλλοισίν τε θεοῖσιν
    And I pray in hope to Zeus and the other gods . . .

    External evidence: 7 mss., according to Allen's *editio maior*.

In the course of a study of the uses of εὔχομαι in Homer,[149] Leonard Muellner deals with these variants,[150] and after detailed argument, concludes that εὔχομαι ἐλπόμενος can possibly be genuine epic diction, although (he claims) it is somewhat more awkward; Zenodotus' reading ἔλπομαι εὐχόμενος is much more easily "defended" by use of parallels. Thus both variants have a right to be considered authentic, and it is not a case of "finding the right one" and discarding the "wrong one."[151]

As an example of how one might deal with variants which are treated as being of equal authenticity, I quote A. di Luzio, who, after examining closely the variants of the Ptolemaic papyri, concludes that they reflect a text not yet normalized, and closer to the fluctuating state of the rhapsodic epic when transmission and "reproduction" of the text were still under the influence of "recitation." This in contrast with the seemingly normalized "vulgate" text, coming from a later time when transmission was due more to the letter and less to the hearing. Di Luzio envisions a critical edition of Homer in which

> equivalent variants do not remain confined to the critical apparatus, but are situated in the margin of the text. Thus the reader could select the reading according to his own taste; and the delight of the choice would not be reserved only for the learned editor.[152]

---

[147] I note Allen's incorrect accentuation of εὔχομενος in the text; it is correct in the critical apparatus.

[148] So Allen changed his mind between 1920 (OCT) and 1931 (*editio maior*).

[149] Muellner 1976.

[150] Ibid., 57ff.

[151] I note that Muellner himself does not come to this conclusion in this particular case: on p. 62 he decides that ἔλπομαι εὐχόμενος is the original, and the other reading results from a scribe's error; rather than that "the tradition produced εὔχομαι ἐλπόμενος from its own repertoire," although he clearly shows that it could have done so.

[152] Luzio 1969. This last quote from p. 151: "In tal modo il lettore potrebbe scegliere la lezione secondo il proprio gusto; e il diletto della scelta non sarebbe riservato solo all'erudito editore."

To return for a moment to biblical textual criticism, I illustrate below (Figure 4) how a similar scheme has been proposed for handling Greek New Testament variants, with the goal of comparing variants with each other, rather than with any supposed "standard."[153] This diagram deals with the variants for the Gospel of John 7:12. (I omit the mss. evidence, which is listed under each reading in the original scheme.)

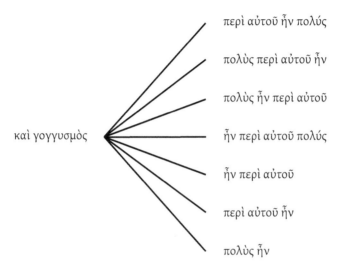

Figure 4. A way of displaying multiple variant readings in "parallel," using John 7:12. From Epp and Fee 1993:79.

As illustrated above, I wish to preserve all available surviving variants (at least those which do not appear to be simple copyists' errors), and present them in, as it were, a parallel fashion, so that the reader can see them as equals, and (to use di Luzio's words) experience the delight of making his/her own choice, or rather, of experiencing firsthand the multiformity that is so much a part of the genre of oral traditional poetry.[154]

In this chapter I have attempted to argue that the Homeric text presents us with a far different situation from that of purely written works, and that we

His goal of defending the "plus verses" of the Ptolemaic papyri is criticized by Apthorp (1980: xxv).

[153] Epp and Fee 1993:79. Several more complex diagrams are also presented there.

[154] Compare also the work of R. T. Pickens in editing a multitext version of the songs of Jaufré Rudel, a twelfth-century Provençal *troubadour*. See above, p. 47n80; also Nagy 1996a:8ff.

must accordingly treat it with significantly different tools and methodologies, freeing ourselves of anachronistic and inappropriate ideas about written textual transmission. By a proper understanding of the theory of oral performance and transmission, we are in a better position to interpret the textual evidence when it presents us with results that appear at first glance to be anomalous or inexplicable. In showing that more than one reading in a given passage can be considered "authentic," whether by demonstrating that it is ancient, or by showing that it is formulaically appropriate, or both, we begin to see that our Homeric textual evidence clearly points toward the reality of "multitextuality."

In the next chapter I look at the Ptolemaic papyri of the *Iliad*, with a view to exploring how some of their "wildest" features—their plus verses coupled with their significant textual variation within lines—can be seen as contributing strong support to the idea of "multitextuality" in the *Iliad*.

Chapter 3

The Ptolemaic Papyri of the *Iliad*:

Evidence of Eccentricity or Multitextuality?

U NTIL THE END OF THE NINETEENTH CENTURY, the text of Homer, as preserved in papyri and medieval manuscripts, was relatively uniform, with few significant variant readings to exercise scholars. True, there were instances where an ancient author such as Plato or Aeschines had quoted a passage of Homer in a way that differed in unusual ways from the "received text," but these cases were generally put down to the faulty memory of the author.

When, however, in 1890 the first Homeric papyrus dating to the Ptolemaic period (P8, containing *Iliad* XI 502–537) was discovered by W. M. Flinders Petrie[1] in Gurob in Egypt and published in 1891 by J. P. Mahaffy,[2] it was found to contain a surprisingly different version of the text: four lines not in the "vulgate" (labeled according to current convention as 504a, 509a, 513a, and 514a), one "missing" line (either 529 or 530), and some significant variation within two existing lines (515 and 520). Further, S. West notes that the variation in line 515 is directly related to the "insertion" of the previous line, 514a.[3] This exemplifies the fact that many "plus verses" are not just "interpolated" randomly into the text; rather they tend to fit "organically"—the surrounding context frequently gives the appearance of having been "modified" to allow them to fit better.[4]

---

[1] See Turner 1968:24. Flinders Petrie himself (1892) gives a fascinating account of the life of a nineteenth-century explorer in Egypt: on p. 3 he mentions the need to "subordinate the stomach to the intellect"; and on p. 12 he describes one of his places of residence as a "tomb"—which it was, literally—adding that in subsequent years, "often when in draughty houses, or chilly tents, I have wished myself back in my tomb."

[2] Mahaffy 1891:33ff. See also S. West 1967:103–107.

[3] S. West, ibid., 106.

[4] Compare the "vertical"/"horizontal" types of variation discussed above, chap. 2, n109. In addition, I note the use of the term "variation units" in Epp and Fee 1993:49–50, to refer to a passage from the Greek New Testament which includes at least two "significant" variant readings, each supported by at least two independent textual witnesses.

As discussed earlier,[5] the manuscripts of Homer may be divided into two basic and broad groups, based on age and the type of material used: papyrus and parchment. However, I note the two following (not necessarily helpful) conventions: the term "papyrus" is taken to mean "any ancient manuscript, whether or not it is written on papyrus," whereas the term "manuscript" means "medieval manuscript."[6] The first of these conventions helps to explain why, for instance, the very first item in the standard list of "papyrus manuscripts" of the *Iliad*, viz. P1 ("codex Ambrosianus," dated 5th–6th century CE), is actually written on parchment (as are P89,[7] P162, and P233). A few further "papyrus" documents, all originally school exercises, are of other materials: limestone inscriptions (e.g. P107, P108, P110 and P121), *ostraka* (e.g. P137, P161, P263, P522, and P525) and wooden tablets (P131 and P164).[8]

Further complicating matters regarding papyrus identification, as the number of "papyri" has grown, the numbering system has been modified somewhat: starting with (for the *Iliad*) T. W. Allen's original P1–P122,[9] the list currently extends as far as P1569 in Martin West's 2001 study, which correlates closely to his 1998 and 2000 *Iliad* editions. West (following Sutton) includes two further categories: first, ancillary documents such as glossaries and scholia minora, notated h1–h142 (the h stands for "Homerica"); second, non-Homeric papyri containing Homeric quotations; these are labeled w1–w47 (the w stands for "witness").[10]

It happens that the distinction between the terms "papyrus" and "manuscript" coincides with a division both of date and of writing style: virtually all the "papyri" date from between the fourth/third century BCE and the eighth century CE, whereas almost all the "manuscripts" are dated from the ninth to the eighteenth centuries CE; similarly, the uncial form of writing is exclusively used on all documents until it is superseded by minuscule script around the ninth century CE. The other major change which takes place is that from roll (or scroll) to codex: rolls tend to die out around the end of the 4th century CE,

---

[5] Above, chap. 2, pp. 30–31.

[6] See Haslam 1997:55n1. He describes this latter habit as "pernicious." See also n15 below for an example of a medieval papyrus manuscript.

[7] T. W. Allen's label; Sutton (see next note), followed by M. L. West, relabels it as "h74."

[8] In this chapter I depend on *Homer in the Papyri: A Computerized Database* (Sutton 1997), and subsequently West 2001:86–138 for a good deal of the information on Homeric papyri.

[9] See Allen 1931 (vol. 1, *Prolegomena*), pp. 1–10. On p. 1 he states that "a complete list of Homeric papyri is not attempted."

[10] See West 2001 for further details on the labeling system. West points out that in his Teubner edition he dispenses with the letter "P" for papyrus in the *apparatus criticus* for the sake of economy; context makes it clear when a papyrus reading is being referred to.

and codices, whose use begins early in the 2nd century (or perhaps earlier), quickly become the standard vehicle.[11]
I illustrate these features in simplified diagrammatic form:

4TH/3RD CENT. BCE–8TH CENT. CE	9TH CENT. CE–18TH CENT. CE
papyrus	parchment
uncial script	minuscule script
scroll/roll and codex	codex

The reasons for the change from papyrus to parchment (i.e. the skins of sheep and goats[12])—and the more significant change from the roll to the codex—involve at least in part convenience and practicality: parchment is longer lasting (except in the deserts of Egypt, where papyrus if kept dry will survive relatively intact), and papyrus was generally far less available. The major benefits to using codices instead of rolls were both convenience to the reader and the increase in the total amount of material that could be contained in a single volume.[13] Advantages of minuscule over uncial script included primarily speed of writing, as well as the use of capitals for proper names and titles.[14]

The earliest *Iliad* papyri date from the fourth/third century BCE, with at present 17 papyri from this period. At the other end of the chronological scale are 27 papyri from the sixth and seventh centuries. Thus *Iliad* papyri span roughly a thousand-year period, from the "Ptolemaic," through the "Roman," and into the "Byzantine" periods. Chart 1 illustrates the distribution of those papyri of the *Iliad* which can be dated (more than four-fifths of the total). One immediately notices the "normal" (in a statistical sense) shape of the graph, indicating among other things the scarcity of Ptolemaic (6 percent) and late Byzantine papyri (12 percent), as well as the relative abundance of Roman texts (82 percent). Whatever the factors responsible for this state of affairs, our examination of the Ptolemaic papyri must bear in mind that our surviving amount of evidence is tiny, and cannot automatically be assumed to be a "representative sample." However, neither can its evidence be ignored. I add for comparison Chart 2, which includes the medieval manuscripts along with the papyri.

---

[11] See Turner 1968. On p. 11 he gives figures showing that rolls are gradually supplanted by codices between the second and fourth centuries CE.

[12] Turner 1968:8–9.

[13] Turner (ibid.) mentions Pliny's account (*Epistles*, II, 1, 5) of the aged Verginius Rufus breaking his hip while trying to pick up a roll he had dropped.

[14] Nagy (2009:139–140) describes how the Venetus A manuscript of the *Iliad* includes in its scholia both uncial and "non-uncial" types of writing; the former preserves older (and hence more accurate) ways of reading the Homeric text aloud.

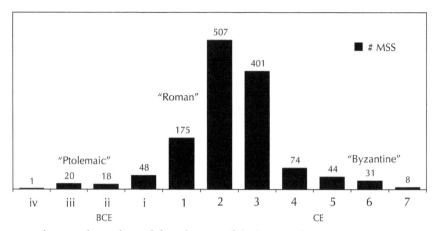

Chart 1. Chronological distribution of *Iliad* papyri, by century.

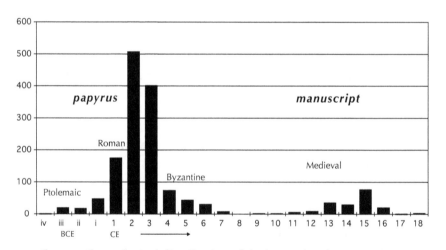

Chart 2. Chronological distribution of *Iliad* papyri and manuscripts, by century.

Note the far smaller number of these later witnesses to the text; however, what the chart does *not* show is that the medieval manuscripts each contain on average far greater amounts of Homeric text; in contrast, some of the papyri are extremely fragmentary, containing sometimes only a few partial lines.

In addition to the more than 1,500 "papyri" of the *Iliad* mentioned above, plus the 142 "Homerica" and the 47 "witnesses," there are 190 medieval (non-papyrus) manuscripts,[15] dating from the ninth to the eighteenth centuries CE.

---

[15] Allen 1931 (*Prolegomena*) 11–55 listed 188; West (2001:139–142) includes the papyrus P568 as "X," along with a further manuscript "Y," which Allen had not used, bringing the total to 190.

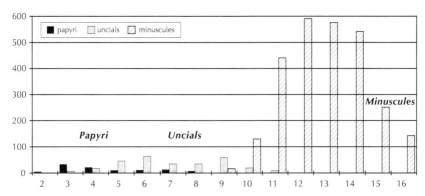

Chart 3. Chronological distribution of Greek New Testament papyri and manuscripts, by century.

The oldest is "X" (not known to Allen), dated to the ninth century CE, and containing portions of text along with an interlinear prose paraphrase. The earliest complete text of the *Iliad* is the famous Venetus A (Marcianus 454, tenth century),[16] and the latest is U[12] (not listed by West), dated to 1752, containing 5 books of the *Iliad*, and "not collated."[17] This gives a total of approximately 1,900[18] surviving documents which bear direct witness to the text of the *Iliad*, with a span of approximately two thousand years.

Finally, as previously mentioned, we have the evidence of the scholia, the classical and post-classical quotations,[19] so-called "allusions"—references to the Homeric text that are not actual quotations but nevertheless indicate a familiarity with the Homeric text[20]—vase paintings,[21] and inscriptions such as those on the Dipylon Vase and "Nestor's Cup."[22]

Of all classical literature Homer, and specifically the *Iliad*, is represented by the largest quantity of manuscript evidence. This is because Homer was read more than any other classical author, both in schools and by the reading public. As I have already noted above, the situation for the Greek New Testament is comparable to that of Homer. I illustrate the manuscript data for the GNT in Chart 3,[23] which makes for an interesting comparison with Chart 2. The fact that

---

I will generally use West's labeling system rather than that of Allen, except where West does not mention a manuscript in Allen's lists.

[16] See Allen 1931:11, 162–166; also Dué 2009.
[17] Allen 1931:43.
[18] See again chap. 1, p. 1.
[19] See esp. Ludwich 1898.
[20] See esp. Garner 1990 and Rengakos 1993.
[21] E.g. Snodgrass 1998.
[22] See Powell 1997:23–24. Both inscriptions include hexameters, and the latter apparently contains a reference to the *Iliad*.
[23] Data from Aland 1987:81–83.

these two charts are virtually mirror images of each other indicates a lot about the very different circumstances of the transmission of the two texts.

I move now to a closer examination of the Ptolemaic papyri of the *Iliad*. The term "Ptolemaic papyri" refers collectively to a group of papyrus manuscripts possessing a common location of discovery and datable to a common period. The general location is Egypt, and the period is that roughly covering the reigns of the first eight Ptolemies—from Ptolemy I Soter, who ruled from 305/304 to 283/282, to Ptolemy VIII (Euergetes II), who ruled intermittently, as well as both solely and jointly, between 170 and his death in 116. There appears to have been some sort of turmoil around the year 146/145, when Ptolemy VIII returned from Cyrene to Egypt and overthrew and killed his nephew Ptolemy VII (Neos Philopator). Included amongst the events of that troubled time was the expulsion from Alexandria of the grammarians, including Aristarchus of Samothrace, of whom more will be said. This date, 146 or 145 BCE, is often considered the end of the Ptolemaic period as far as the "eccentric" papyri are concerned, for reasons which will be discussed; however Grenfell and Hunt state that the Ptolemaic period ends in 30 BCE, as in the listing below:[24]

Ptolemaic	before 30 BCE
Roman	30 BCE–284 CE
Early Byzantine	284–400 CE
Late Byzantine	after 400 CE

For the purposes of this chapter, I use the following simplified scheme for manuscripts (papyrus or otherwise):

Ptolemaic	iii–i	(i.e. third to first centuries BCE)
Roman	I–III	(i.e. first to third centuries CE)
Byzantine	IV–VIII	(i.e. fourth to eighth centuries CE)

In this chapter I will note the significance of the date 146/145, while also considering papyri that date as late as the end of the first century BCE.

The Ptolemaic papyri of Homer, the first of which[25] was published in 1891 and the most recent[26] in 1984, aroused a great deal of excitement when they first saw the light, evoking various reactions and theories from scholars; some of these theories did not last long, while others are still held today.

---

[24] Grenfell and Hunt 1906.
[25] P8, containing about 36 lines from *Iliad* XI. See below, p. 70.
[26] P609, containing portions of *Iliad* X. Another papyrus, P662, containing a few lines from *Iliad* XIX, was originally (in 1922) edited as a fragment of Euripides, but subsequently (in 1989) identified and reedited as Homeric.

Descriptions of the painstaking work involved, the frustration of finding a tiny fragment of some work, and the knowledge that the vast majority of fragments are forever lost, make compelling reading and cause one both to admire the diligence of these early explorers, and to value more highly those pieces which do survive.

Almost all surviving classical papyri (and those of the Hebrew Bible and the Greek New Testament) come from Egypt, south of the Delta, where the rainless climate favors their survival.[27] In general the vast majority of papyri come from ruined buildings and from the rubbish dumps of villages in Upper (i.e. southern) Egypt.[28] Some have been found in tombs, some were buried in jars, and some have been extracted from the wrappings of mummies. Those papyri that fall into this last category bear the description "cartonnage." J. P. Mahaffy describes how at one of the sites, Gurob, coffins were "made of layers of papyrus, torn into small pieces, and stuck together so as to form a thick carton, painted within and without with designs and religious emblems."[29] The man who discovered the first Ptolemaic papyrus of Homer, Flinders Petrie, detected in the structure of these cartons the use of discarded documents, and began the task of separating and cleaning the fragments. Difficulties included the fact that often chalk had been used to draw on the surface of the papyrus, thereby destroying the ink; also worms would bore into the papyrus in search of the glue which was used to join papyrus strips; and sometimes "soaking the fragments in water releases a substance which irreparably stains what is left of any writing on the papyrus."[30]

The names of Grenfell and Hunt, who discovered more Ptolemaic papyri of Homer than anyone else (including the "eccentric" P7, P12, P40, and P41), are almost synonymous with papyrological discovery. They too give an account of some of their experiences, an account which underlines the tenuousness of the element of chance in searching for and finding papyrus documents.[31] The mummies, wrapped in cartonnage made out of papyrus fragments, were buried anywhere from a few inches to several feet below the surface of the ground. In some of the deeper cases, the original burial sites were covered with a layer of debris from the Roman period. For such papyrus fragments to survive, there had to be a total lack of moisture; and since we are dealing with

---

[27] Exceptions include: the Epicurean papyri from Herculaneum; Hellenistic and Roman documents from Dura-Europos; papyri from Qumran ("Dead Sea Scrolls"), Murabba'at, and Auja-el-Hafir; and the Homeric "w38"—an Orphic papyrus from Derveni near Thessaloniki.
[28] See Maehler 1996:1109–1111.
[29] Mahaffy 1891:9.
[30] Ibid.
[31] Grenfell and Hunt 1906:1–12.

a desert, through the middle of which flows a river (the Nile), all towns and villages were (and largely still are) very close to the water. We have the paradoxical situation of the Nile being the place where all the papyri are located, but also being one of the greatest threats to their survival. Thus a large amount of papyrus material will have been lost due to moisture damage, and Grenfell and Hunt comment on this in their account.[32]

In addition to staying dry for well over two thousand years, the papyri had to have escaped plundering, both ancient and modern, by local inhabitants and looters. In their search for more valuable artifacts, these "explorers" originally discarded cartonnage as being of no value, and only later learned that it was to their advantage to preserve it. In some cases the "locals," all too aware of the value of individual fragments, would even separate pieces of papyrus so as to sell them separately for more money than the original larger piece would have fetched.[33] Thus a significant part of the process of editing a papyrus consists of deciding which pieces come from the same original manuscript, and then attempting to join or at least locate such pieces in their original position—rather like a jigsaw puzzle for which only a fraction of the pieces are available. For example, Stephanie West's edition of P12 (the longest Ptolemaic papyrus of Homer) consists of at least thirty "large" recognizable pieces, plus more than forty smaller, unidentifiable fragments.[34]

Provenance is not always easy or even possible to determine; Grenfell and Hunt remark that some of their papyrus fragments came to them by means of a dealer, far from where they had been unearthed, while others they uncovered themselves. Opposite is a table showing the number of papyri of the *Iliad* for which the provenance is fairly certain (373 out of about 1,900, or approximately one-fifth). I separate the Ptolemaic papyri from the rest; note the importance of Hibeh, thanks in large part to the team of Grenfell and Hunt.

Even in cases where the provenance is known, one cannot be sure that the papyrus was actually written there. Either the papyrus or the mummy (or both) could have been transported from elsewhere. External evidence is thus often lacking, but on occasion an intact mummy contains a datable and/or locatable fragment; this is of great assistance in dating/locating other fragments attached to the same mummy. Sometimes a group of mummies found in close proximity contain parts of the same papyrus document.[35] Mahaffy

---

[32] Grenfell and Hunt 1906:4.
[33] Mahaffy (1891:2) blames the "vulgar tourist" for "lavishing money ignorantly and at random" and thus "encouraging the natives to maximize their profits."
[34] S. West 1967:136–154.
[35] Grenfell and Hunt 1906:11.

Numbers of *Iliad* Papyri with Secure Provenance

Site	Ptolemaic	Later	Total
Oxyrhynchus	–	200	200
Fayum	2	31	33
Hermupolis	–	28	28
Tebtunis	4	20	24
Soknopaiou Nesos	–	10	10
Hibeh	8	1	9
Karanis	1	8	9
Madinet Madi	–	9	9
Theadelphia	–	7	7
Thebes	–	7	7
Gurob	1	–	1
El Lahoun	1	–	1
Magdola	1	–	1
other	–	34	34
TOTALS	18	355	373

describes how he (along with Petrie and A. H. Sayce) was "arrested and sur-prised" to find that the papyrus fragments they were cleaning and deci-phering included legal documents which mentioned, instead of the expected late Ptolemies or Roman emperors (as in previously found documents), the names of the second and third Ptolemies—i.e. the materials could be dated no later than 220 BCE, and therefore the classical texts mixed up with these docu-ments were themselves most likely to be of such an early date.[36]

Grenfell and Hunt conclude that in the case of the Hibeh papyri, much of the material for the cartonnage originated from a library of classical literature, probably belonging to a Greek settler at Oxyrhynchus, which is some thirty to forty miles southwest of Hibeh, on the opposite (west) bank of the Nile.[37]

It needs to be stressed that Homeric Ptolemaic papyri make up only a tiny fraction of the total papyri of the Ptolemaic period—the majority are admin-istrative documents, and several are of other classical authors. Some are obvi-ously classical and literary but so far not identified as to author. Nonetheless our small numbers of Homeric papyri, when used with proper precautions

[36] Mahaffy 1891:11.
[37] Grenfell and Hunt 1906:12.

Chapter 3

(to be discussed below), are invaluable for the light they shed on the text of Homer at this period and, I hope to argue, at earlier times as well.[38]

As mentioned above, the discovery of the Ptolemaic papyri of Homer aroused great curiosity and excitement initially. By the year 1897 the following *Iliad* papyri had been unearthed, all dating to the third century BCE:

Ptolemaic Papyri of the *Iliad* Recovered by 1897 (all 3rd century BCE)

Papyrus	No. lines	"New" lines	Percent	Provenance	Discoverer	Date*	Source
P8	36	5	13.9%	Gurob	F. Petrie	1891	cartonnage
P5	72	9	12.5%	??	J. Nicole	1894	??
P7	~90	31?	34.4%	Hibeh	G. & H.**	1897	cartonnage
P12	~282	27?	9.6%	Hibeh	G. & H.	1897	cartonnage
P41	73	1	1.4%	Hibeh	G. & H.	1897	cartonnage

* This is the date of publication, not necessarily of original discovery.
** Grenfell and Hunt 1906.

The column labeled "percent" is calculated by dividing the number of new lines by the number of lines in total—i.e. dividing column 3 by column 2. Thus for P7 one can see that 33%, or approximately 1 in 3 of its lines are "new"—i.e. not in our "usual" text of Homer.

T. W. Allen,[39] reviewing (favorably) Arthur Ludwich's *Die Homervulgata als voralexandrinisch erwiesen* (Leipzig 1898), describes how until 1891 the manuscripts of Homer were fairly homogeneous, presenting the "vulgate," although contrasting at times with each of the other two types of evidence, viz. the scholia and the quotations. Then between 1891 and 1897 the five papyri listed above were discovered, with their "remarkable variants," in particular additions to the "ordinary" text.

Two theories were initially put forward:[40] first, that the Ptolemaic papyri represent the pre-Alexandrian state of the text, which became the vulgate through the work of Zenodotus et al. This was soon shown to be untenable, as the Alexandrians' readings seldom coincide with the text of the "vulgate." The second theory suggested that the Ptolemaic papyri prove that the vulgate

[38] S. West (1967) edits and comments on those Ptolemaic papyri of Homer available up to 1965; for papyri after that date I have depended upon the computerized database of D. F. Sutton, and subsequently West 2001 (see above, n8).
[39] Allen 1899.
[40] See Grenfell and Hunt 1906:67–75.

70

cannot yet have been in existence, but rather that there were several versions of the text in varying degrees of circulation. Ludwich's own theory, as his title indicates, was that our "vulgate" in fact dates back to a pre-Alexandrian date.

Allen also warns us in this article not to be overly impressed by the striking nature of the "plus verses," because of the extremely tiny size of the corpus (see below). Nevertheless, Allen considers the chief advance to be that "the Ptolemaic papyri do *confirm the quotations"* (Allen's emphasis)—i.e. classical authors such as Plato (*2nd Alcibiades*) and Aeschines (*Against Timarchus*) seem now not to have been quoting from a faulty memory, and critics who in the past felt justified in disregarding such quotations were now forced to look at them in a more serious light. In two cases (out of the then-extant Ptolemaic fragments), Plato and Aeschines can be shown to have quoted from extant versions of the text rather than from an imperfect recollection of the "original."[41] Similarly, because of supporting evidence in the Ptolemaic papyri, Allen pronounces that "Plutarch's accuracy is therefore vindicated; he verified his references," and hence "it must follow that quotations are to be treated with more respect than heretofore." Allen uses the term "eccentric" in this article—in a later work he claims to be the first to have done so.[42]

I note here the caveats of two scholars concerning the chance nature of what survives and what has perished. In the 1899 article just discussed, T. W. Allen warned that much of what survives in the way of papyrus material has been subject to the capriciousness of chance; since at that time there were so few (although the number was regularly increasing) Ptolemaic papyri of Homer, he cautioned against making confident assertions about how things were, based on the slim body of evidence.[43] In another place he mentions the "capricious evidence," and asks rhetorically, "Herodotus in 11 quoted lines (from different places) has no additional lines, but what if he had quoted 100 continuous lines?"[44] In a similar vein Turner warns of the "element of chance" regarding what has been discovered, and where. Just because no papyri have been found at Alexandria, one should resist the temptation to conclude that there never were any. "The case of Alexandria illustrates the unpredictability of papyrus evidence. Almost anything may turn up, yet what is expected often

---

[41] See e.g. Dué 2001, demonstrating that the text of Aeschines' *Against Timarchus*—which contains an extended Homeric quotation differing from the "vulgate" text—is supported by P12, a Ptolemaic papyrus which covers some of the same lines.

[42] Allen 1924:302.

[43] Allen 1899:39: "the enormous working of the element of chance."

[44] Allen 1924:249–269.

does not seem to. From such finds one may argue positively but not negatively: the argument from silence is especially dangerous."[45]

As I have discussed frequently in this book, most scholars appear to work from the assumption that there was an "original" text of the *Iliad*, from which manuscripts such as the Ptolemaic papyri "deviated" more or less significantly; therefore terms such as "correct" and "incorrect" or "genuine" and "spurious" are frequently encountered in the literature dealing with textual matters. In Chapter Two I examined this and similar assumptions; at this point I notice how West herself deals with the unusual variations presented by the Ptolemaic papyri. These variations include both significantly different versions of the same line, and—the most unusual feature, and the one which gave rise to descriptions such as "wild" and "eccentric"—the so-called "additional lines" or "plus verses." As Stephanie West states in her introduction, these variants "cannot be explained by the processes of merely mechanical corruption."[46] In the case of an author whose work was written down from the start, one usually has to assume such "processes of mechanical corruption"—the study of which involves application of the science of textual criticism, discussed in Chapters One and Two.

In her preface, West does appear to be "neutral" regarding the Ptolemaic variants:

> The textual criticism of the Homeric poems is perpetually bedevilled by the metaphysics of the Homeric question. It may be no more than wishful thinking to suppose that in any particular case we can arrive at the word or phrase chosen by the monumental composer: perhaps terms like "original" and "authentic" are only relative. For this reason I have often been non-committal, perhaps even cursory, in discussing the variants offered by these papyri.[47]

Further on, in her introduction, she states

> There is no evidence that . . . [there was] anything abnormal about these texts; . . . Plato and Aeschines . . . used very similar texts.[48]

With regard to the "plus verses," so frequent in these papyri:

---

[45] Turner 1968:42–50. Also his statements about the "capricious nature of finds at a single site," and the fact of "the accidental wanderings of papyri . . . papyri travel easily from place to place."
[46] S. West 1967:11.
[47] Ibid., 5–6.
[48] Ibid., 11.

There remains a large number of lines for which no close parallel can be found: some of these may have been composed for interpolation, but it is equally possible that they come from lost hexameter poetry.[49]

Here West seems to be torn between the conventional view that lines can be either "genuine" or "interpolated," and the view for which I am arguing in this book, namely that such "additional" lines may indeed be "authentic"—i.e. composed and performed in the oral tradition, and recorded in some texts and not others, because performed on some occasions and not on others. However, West finally concludes,

The relatively minor scale of the interpolations argues against the view that there is a connection between the eccentricities of the early texts and the long oral tradition of the poems, except insofar as the rather discursive style suitable for oral technique attracted interpolation.[50]

As one reads through West's text and commentary, one frequently comes across the following characterizations of papyrus variants (this is only a sample):[51]

I 108	the papyrus' reading is "not inferior."
I 567	the papyrus' reading is "not an aberration."
II 622	the papyrus variant is "not formulaic, may be right."
II 795	the papyrus reading is "superior."
XI 271	both readings [i.e. papyrus and "vulgate"] seem "equally good."
XII 180	the papyrus reading "is not derived from the vulgate," i.e. it is "independent."
XII 183a[52]	it is "very tempting to regard the text of the papyrus as authentic."
XII 192	the papyrus "may well preserve an earlier version of this line."

However one also meets this kind of evaluation:

| XXI 406 | the papyrus presents a "rather stupid variant." |

---

[49] Ibid., 13.
[50] Ibid. Cf. p. 26: "our papyri are riddled with secondary variants and conjectures."
[51] These quotations are taken from the places in her commentary on the lines in question.
[52] This is the standard notation for a "plus verse"—see below.

XXI 412   the papyrus' reading is "worthless."

The point of mentioning these examples is to show that, in spite of appearing to be working from the assumption of one "original" and "genuine" text of the *Iliad*, West is still willing at times to allow for the "authenticity" of a papyrus reading, and even for the equal value of more than one variant. I argue later in this chapter that one can and should go further, showing that there are many cases where both the papyrus and the "vulgate" reading (and sometimes the reading of Zenodotus or Aristarchus as well) can be demonstrated—often by both internal and external evidence—to be "authentic," i.e. that the passage is "Homeric" whichever variant is read.

I note here briefly the views of some other scholars regarding the usefulness or otherwise of the Ptolemaic papyri of Homer. M. van der Valk, in his chapter dealing with the Homeric papyri, writes that

> most modern critics take the view that especially the early Ptolemaic papyri make it clear that originally, in the fourth and third centuries BCE, the Homeric text was uncertain and different versions of it existed.[53]

Van der Valk himself, however, is convinced that "in most instances the papyri are wrong over against the mss."[54] In suitably dramatic language he proclaims his lonely and lowly[55] position amidst a host of scholars who seem all too ready to "fall on th[eir] knees before the papyri."[56]

E. G. Turner[57] notes the view (held by, for example, G. Jachmann) that some "plus verses" actually improve the Homeric style of the passage (e.g. *Iliad* XII 189–193). He points out that this type of divergence cannot be put down to "mere carelessness by the scribe," but adds that it reflects rather "a lack of respect for the accurate recording of an author's words." He contrasts this attitude—that the exact words of an author are not sacred and hence do not need to be copied verbatim—with the later Roman mindset that encouraged more of a "respect for the authority of the text," a respect which he largely credits to the Alexandrians.[58] And yet he allows for the good textual basis of at least some of these "wild" papyri, warning us not to dismiss them as "the

---

[53] Van der Valk 1964:531.
[54] Ibid. I notice his similar evaluations of the work of Zenodotus and Aristarchus.
[55] He likens himself to a common soldier trying to advise a general.
[56] Ibid., 532n6, modifying a statement of Lehrs.
[57] Turner 1986:107.
[58] Ibid., 108.

property of uneducated immigrants and untypical. They are beautiful examples of calligraphy, and they contain good readings as well as a high coefficient of error and a high proportion of change."[59] So Turner also, like West, is willing to grant some value to the readings of these papyri, while still insisting that much of their variation is due to what might called today a "fast and loose" approach to the text.

G. S. Kirk[60] and R. Janko[61] take basically the same view as S. West, and also (like van der Valk) minimize the value of the work of the Alexandrians in their efforts to find the "original" text of Homer. Taking a contrary position is G. Nagy, who attributes significant value both to the readings of the Ptolemaic papyri and to the work of the Alexandrian scholars.[62]

As mentioned above, one of the most unusual features of the Ptolemaic papyri, and the one which aroused the most interest when the documents were first discovered, is that of the "plus verses," i.e. the relatively large number of cases where extra lines appeared to be inserted into otherwise familiar passages of the *Iliad* and *Odyssey*. By way of illustration, I include on the next few pages a set of tables showing the frequency of "plus verses" in papyri from the fourth/third to the first centuries BCE, i.e. during the Ptolemaic period. The data are taken from T. W. Allen,[63] with my corrections, and additions from S. West,[64] D. F. Sutton,[65] and M. L. West.[66] The datings are approximate, based on paleographical criteria as well as the external evidence of datable documents discovered in close proximity to the papyrus in question. In some cases the total number of lines or the number of new lines ("plus verses") is uncertain as a result of the poor condition of the papyrus fragment. In addition S. West lists many fragments that cannot with any degree of certainty be matched up with an existing Ptolemaic papyrus; there is always the possibility that more "plus verses" or other significant variants are lurking just behind the scenes.

---

[59] Ibid. I note Turner's frequent use of the term "wild" in this context.
[60] E.g. Kirk 1985:43.
[61] E.g. Janko 1992:22.
[62] Nagy 1996a, chap. 5.
[63] Allen 1931.I:91.
[64] S. West 1967.
[65] Sutton 1997.
[66] West 2001.

"New" Lines in the Ptolemaic Papyri of the *Iliad*

4th/3rd century BCE

Papyrus	Book(s)	No. lines	"New" lines	Percent
w38*	24	2	0	–
P5	11–12	72	11	15.3%
P7	8	90	32	35.6%
P8	11	36	4	11.1%
P12	21–23	282	28	9.9%
P59	16	6	0	–
P410	6	4	0	–
P432	11–12	64	14	21.9%
P480a	6	13	3	23.1%
P496	12	31	0	–
P501c**	17	17	4	23.5%
P672	17	15	1	6.7%
h59*** (quotation)	6	8	0	–
h117^ (anthology)	3	6	2	33.3%
h125^^ (quotation)	2	9	0	–
w14^^^ (quotation)	2, 5, 9, 13	8?	1?	12.5%
w19 (commentary)	4, 5, 14	3	0	–
TOTALS		666	100	15.0%

* This is the only fourth-century papyrus: it quotes 2 lines of *Iliad* XXIV as Orpheus.
** P501c is dated by Sutton and West as "Ptolemaic."
*** Previously labeled P317.
^ Previously labeled P. Mich. 5.
^^ Previously labeled P459.
^^^ Previously labeled P. Hamb. 137.

3rd–2nd century BCE

Papyrus	Book(s)	No. lines	"New" lines	Percent
P40	2–3	95	14	14.7%
P269	1	26	1	3.8%
P391	3	10	0	–
P494	10	16	0	–
P590	7	13	0	–
P593	8	15	0	–
P662	19	5	0	–
h103	glosses	–	–	–
TOTALS		180	15	8.3%

2nd century BCE

Papyrus	Book(s)	No. lines	"New" lines	Percent
P41	3–5	73	1	1.4%
P37	2	116	0	–
P53	1	12	2	16.7%
P217	12	90	8	8.9%
P266	1	8	0	–
P354	1	45	2	4.4%
P460	2	14	0	–
P609	10	30	1	3.3%
h68 (commentary)	9	19?	0	–
h102 (lexicon)	–	–	–	–
w21 (quotation)	4	1	0	–
TOTALS		408	14	3.4%

2nd–1st century BCE

Papyrus	Book(s)	No. lines	"New" lines	Percent
P102	5	15	0	–
P270	6	297	0	–
P271	22	52	0	–
P333	1	13	0	–
P671	16	35	0	–
h88 (anth./summary)	18–19	–	–	–
TOTALS		412	0	0.0%

1st century BCE

Papyrus	Book(s)	No. lines	"New" lines	Percent
P13	23–24	1,069	3	0.3%
P29	2	9	0	–
P45	23	15	0	–
P47	13	179	0	–
P51	18	13	5	38.5%
30 other papyri		~900	0	–
TOTALS		~2,100	8	0.4%

1st century BCE–1st century CE

Papyrus	Book(s)	No. lines	"New" lines	Percent
20 papyri		440	0	–
TOTALS		440	0	0.0%

I summarize by giving figures again for each of the six time periods:

Century	No. lines	"New" lines	Percent
4th/3rd	666	100	15.0%
3rd–2nd	180	15	8.3%
2nd	408	14	3.4%
2nd–1st	412	0	0.0%
1st	~2,100	8	0.4%
1st BCE–1st CE	440	0	0.0%

As one surveys the tables, the general trend is clear: papyri at the beginning of the Ptolemaic period show a distinct tendency to contain "additional" lines; this tendency diminishes as we proceed from the fourth/third century until we reach the period BCE/CE, when, apart from two papyri (P13 and P51), the "plus verse" phenomenon has virtually disappeared. The departure of Aristarchus from the library at Alexandria (around 146/145 BCE) roughly coincides with the virtual disappearance of the "plus verses"; these two events are generally believed to be related. Although this date (146/145 BCE) does indeed appear to be a terminus, two papyri of the first century BCE contain "plus verses, "and two additional papyri of this period (P53 and P354) are considered "eccentric" by S. West because of significant variants.[67] Conversely, she lists 22 "Vulgate Ptolemaic papyri" of the Iliad (in an appendix on pp. 283–284). However all of these date from after 150 BCE. So it appears that all Iliad papyri which date before 150 CE have "eccentricities" of some sort—unusual variants and/or "plus verses"—while very few later than this date do.

Next I give a complete list of "plus verses" and "minus verses"[68] for the Iliad as presented by the Ptolemaic papyri.[69] "Plus verses" are usually labeled following the last "known" line, starting with a, b, c, etc. "Plus verses" preceding a known line are labeled with x, y, z. One immediately distinguishes those books having the largest numbers of "plus verses": III, VIII, XI, XII, and XXIII (and also those books with none), and an obvious question arises: were these books somehow more likely to "attract" "plus verses" (so West with reference to book VIII[70])? But we also have to keep in mind the comments of Allen and Turner about the vagaries of chance. Maybe if we had more Ptolemaic papyri, the "plus verses" would be more evenly spread.

[67] S. West 1967:15.
[68] A small number of lines that are in the "vulgate" text but are omitted in a Ptolemaic papyrus.
[69] Data based on S. West, D. F. Sutton, and M. L. West.
[70] S. West 1967:75. But the distribution chart below, pp. 82–83, indicates a different answer.

Ptolemaic "Plus Verses" by Book (*Iliad*)

Book	No. +Verses	Location (=Line)	Papyrus	No. −Verses	Location (=Line)	Papyrus
I	+3	484yz	P53	0		
		543a	P269			
II	+4	794a, 855ab	P40	0		
		848a	w14			
III	+13	283a, 302abcd,	P40	−2	133	P391
		304a, 339abc,			389	P41
		362a, 366a				
		425a, 429a	h117			
IV	+1	69a	P41	−1	89[a]	P41
V	0			−1	527	P41
VI	+3	280a, 288ab	P480a	0		
VII	0			0		
VIII	+32?	38a, 52abcd,	P7	−1	6	P593
		54abcd, 55abcd,				
		65abcd ... i, 197a,				
		199a, 202ab, 204a,				
		206a?,[b] 216a,				
		252ab, 255a				
IX	0			0		
X	+1	433a	P609	0		
XI	+24	266abcd, 266yz,	P432	−4	281–283[c]	P432
		272a, 280ab				
		504a, 509a, 513a,	P8		529 or 530[d]	
		514a				
		795ab, 804a, 805a,	P5			
		807a, 827abc,				
		834ab,[e] 840a				
XII	+10[f]	130a, 189b,[g] 190a,	P432	−6		
		193a				

[a] Also omitted by Zenodotus.

[b] Either a "plus verse" or a different version of 207 (S. West 1967:89).

[c] XI 281–283 omitted by P432. S. West (1967:98) thinks that P432 may be "genuine" in omitting these lines.

[d] See S. West 1967:104, 107. There appears to be one line missing between 528 and 531.

[e] "There must have been at least two plus verses here" (S. West 1967:117).

[f] I count only once each the two "plus verses" 189b and 190a, which occur in both papyri.

[g] 189a is not preserved in P432, but is in P217.

.

Ptolemaic "Plus Verses" by Book (*Iliad*) [*cont.*]

Book	No. +Verses	Location (=Line)	Papyrus	No. −Verses	Location (=Line)	Papyrus
XII		183a, 189ab, 190a, 250a, 360a, 363a, 370a	P217[h]		184–187[i] 369, 403	P217
XIII	0			0		
XIV	0			0		
XV	0			0		
XVI	0			0		
XVII	+5	574ab, 578ab 683a	P501c P672	0		
XVIII	+5+[j]	606a, 608abcd	P51[k]	0		
XIX	0			0		
XX	0			0		
XXI	+1	382a	P12[m]	−2	402, 405	P12
XXII	+8	99a, 126a, 259ab, 316abc, 392a	P12	−3/−6?	see note[n]	P12
XXIII	+22	93a, 94a, 130a, 136a, 155a 160a, 162a, 165a, 171a, 172ab 183a, 195a, 209a, 221a, 223ab, 278ab	P12	−1	92[o]	P12
		757abc	P13[p]			
XXIV	0			0		
Totals	+132			−21/−24		

[h] Formerly labeled as P121 and P342.

[i] S. West (1967:124) thinks the papyrus is "genuine" in omitting lines 184–187.

[j] "There must also have been some plus verses between 589 and 596" (West 1967:132). This papyrus contains critical signs next to some lines.

[k] P51 is dated after 150 BCE, but is still considered "Ptolemaic."

[m] West 1967:137: "A second, rather cursive, hand has . . . inserted variants . . . [perhaps] a selection from various texts, a kind of primitive *apparatus criticus*." Some marginal signs.

[n] Perhaps lines XXII 74–76 omitted. XXII 133–135 omitted, inserted after XXII 316.22.

[o] Line 92 was also athetized by Aristarchus. "This is the only place where an ancient athetesis corresponds to an omission in a pre-Aristarchean papyrus" (S. West 1967:171).

[p] P13 is dated after 150 BCE, but is still considered "Ptolemaic."

The purpose of these tables is not to blind the reader with numerical data, but rather to attempt to show one of the most significant features of the Ptolemaic papyri—their "expansiveness" with regard to the "numerus versuum"[71] of the vulgate; these "plus verses," taken as a whole, amount to around three-quarters of a percent of the total lines of the "vulgate" text of the *Iliad*. In the next section I will systematically analyze a good number of these, showing, as many scholars have already recognized, that they can by no means be lumped together as careless or forgetful alterations to the standard text. I will in particular be looking at the surrounding contexts of many of the "plus verses," showing how, rather than being "inserted" arbitrarily into the text, they have rather "grown" into their current positions, resulting in an "organic"and—I argue—"authentic" alternative to our more familiar version. In other words, the two main types of textual variation, "vertical" and "horizontal,"[72] tend to occur in concert much of the time, suggesting strongly that "plus verses" are part of a larger phenomenon, namely the tendency of oral transmission to both vary and expand (and occasionally contract) a portion of the *Iliad* in the midst of a performance.

I conclude this section with one more graphic illustration of the distribution of the Ptolemaic "plus (and minus) verses" in the *Iliad*. On the following pages I show how the "plus and minus verses" are distributed throughout the *Iliad*. Each "cell" represents a 25-line block of text;[73] the darker shading represents parts of the *Iliad* covered—even if very fragmentarily—by one or more Ptolemaic papyri dating to before 150 BCE. The lighter shading represents passages covered by later Ptolemaic papyri—down to the end of the first century BCE. Within these blocks, "plus verses" are marked with a "+" and "minus verses" with a "–". What is significant from these charts is, first, how little of the *Iliad* is actually represented by papyri of the earlier or later Ptolemaic period—none of books IX, XIV, and XX, and very little of books XVI and XIX. Second, the "plus and minus verses" are almost exclusively confined to the earlier Ptolemaic period, specifically the time before the mid second century, the date when it is supposed that Aristarchus was compelled to leave the library at Alexandria. The charts further indicate, contrary to S. West's suggestion (above, n70), that the books containing relatively high proportions of "plus verses" are just those which happen to have a high degree of "coverage," rather than that they are somehow more likely to "attract" "plus

---

[71] See e.g. Nagy 2004:35–37 and 52–55.
[72] See above, n4.
[73] I note that similarly each page of the Venetus A manuscript generally contains 25 lines of Homeric text.

Totals of *Iliad* Plus and Minus Verses

Line/Bk	A	B	Γ	Δ	E	Z	H	Θ	I	K	Λ	M
1–25								−				
26–50								+				
51–75				+				+++++ +++++ +++++ +++++ +				
76–100				−								
101–125												
126–150			−−									+
151–175												
176–200								++				+++++ −−−−
201–225								+++++				
226–250												+
251–275								+++			+++++ ++	
276–300			+			+++					++ −−−	
301–325		+++++										
326–350		+++										
351–375		++										+++
376–400		−										
401–425		+										−
426–450		+								+		
451–475												
476–500	++											
501–525											++++	
526–550	+				−						−	
551–575												
576–600												
601–625												
626–650												
651–675												
676–700												
701–725												
726–750												
751–775												
776–800		+									++	
801–825											+++	
826–850		+									+++++ +	
851–875		++										
876–900												
901–925												
+ (−) vs.	3	4	13 (2)	1 (1)	0 (1)	3	0	32 (1)	0	1	24 (4)	10 (6)

Earlier Ptolemaic papyri (down to mid 2nd century BCE).
Later Ptolemaic papyri (down to 1st century BCE).

Line/Bk	N	Ξ	O	Π	P	Σ	T	Y	Φ	X	Ψ	Ω
1–25												
26–50												
51–75										– –		
76–100										+ –	++ –	
101–125												
126–150										+ – – –	++	
151–175											+++++ ++	
176–200											++	
201–225											++++	
226–250												
251–275										++		
276–300											++	
301–325										+++		
326–350												
351–375												
376–400									+	+		
401–425									– –			
426–450												
451–475												
476–500												
501–525												
526–550												
551–575					++							
576–600					++							
601–625						+++++						
626–650												
651–675												
676–700					+							
701–725												
726–750												
751–775											+++	
776–800												
801–825												
826–850												
851–875												
876–900												
901–925												
+ (–) vs.	0	0	0	0	5	*5	0	0	1 (2)	8 (6)	*22 (1)	0

verses" because of their content and style. The asterisks next to the totals for books XVIII and XXIII refer to the two papyri dating from after 150 BCE that contain "plus verses."

The charts should be read with their inherent limitations borne in mind: no indication is given of the condition of the individual papyri, nor of the fraction of each line preserved. In most cases lines do not survive in their entirety, but rather just their beginnings, ends, or middles; sometimes only one or two letters, and at times just an empty space indicating that there must have been one or more "plus verses."[74] Often there are fragments from the same original roll, with the intervening portion lost. But in spite of this, the main point I think holds: "plus verses"—at least the type found in the Ptolemaic papyri—are a uniquely early phenomenon, and reflect a distinctively different way in which the text of the *Iliad* was "behaving" at that time. I pursue this further now in the next section.

An Examination of Some Ptolemaic Papyrus Passages

In this section I look closely at a selection of passages from the Ptolemaic papyri, focusing primarily on "plus verses," but also examining the surrounding context of these unfamiliar lines, and looking at how, far from being simply "inserted" arbitrarily into Homeric episodes, these lines seem to fit "organically" into their locations.

My procedure will be first to give the immediate context of the passage in question, then to give the "vulgate" Greek text along with a fairly literal translation into English, and then provide the papyrus Greek text and translation. I then give an analysis of the papyrus text. I sometimes give more lines for context than there are in the papyrus, as papyri are so often torn at an inconvenient place in the text.

I follow several somewhat arbitrary but generally accepted conventions. I print both texts with lowercase script except for proper names; accents and breathing marks, including in reconstructed portions of text; iota adscript instead of subscript; and the two forms of lowercase sigma. Square brackets ([ ]) indicate where the papyrus has been torn away; a dot under a letter indicates that its reading is not certain. Sometimes there is an extended portion of a line where no letters can be made out; in such a case the space will be either blank or filled with dots, corresponding roughly to the number of "missing" letters. In these cases I also bracket the English translation, as an approximate

---

[74] See above, pp. 79–80, table notes e and j.

way of showing how much (but rarely which actual Greek words) of a particular line is missing in the papyrus.

For the "vulgate" text I use Martin West's new Teubner edition of the *Iliad*, not to imply that he has slavishly followed the medieval manuscript tradition—indeed he frequently chooses "non-vulgate" readings, sometimes readings of one of the Alexandrians, sometimes scholarly conjectures, and sometimes a reading preserved by only a small number of witnesses. And as said previously in this book, his respect for the papyri—indicated by always citing their readings first—is much appreciated by those of us with an interest in papyri. I use West's text as the "standard" against which I compare the Ptolemaic papyrus readings.[75] This may seem like a contradiction to my stated aims, which include the principle that in cases where multiple variants exist, no one reading should automatically be privileged above all the others. However, I follow this procedure in the interests of practicality, and because, as people have generally viewed the texts of the Ptolemaic papyri as unusual or "wild" or "eccentric," I treat them, at least initially, as "marked" (in the linguistic sense of that term), meaning that there needs to be a corresponding "unmarked" or "default" text. My goal is to show, as has been acknowledged by S. West among others, that at one time these texts were no more unusual than any others of their time period. So my aim will be to demonstrate that the Ptolemaic papyrus readings are often as "good" or "authentic" as the "default" text.

I indicate where the papyrus reading differs from the Teubner by underlining all differences, including any "plus verses," and this both in the Greek and in the English. This allows the reader to see easily not only the "plus verses," but also how much other variation there is in the immediate context. Of course we cannot always be certain of the correctness of a particular reconstruction—it is quite possible that if we had more of a particular line of a papyrus surviving, it might differ substantially from our current conjecture, hence resulting in a papyrus even more "eccentric" than we had previously supposed.

Needless to say, my "defense" of some of these seemingly "eccentric" readings is not going to change the mind of anyone who has already decided in advance, as evidently had Bolling and van der Valk, that there could never be more than one "correct" reading in a given passage. But for those who have come to agree with Parry and Lord's understanding of oral poetry, its compo-

---

[75] I will use the term "Teubner" (or sometimes "vulgate") whenever I am quoting from West's edition.

sition, performance, and transmission, the following analyses should seem hardly surprising or threatening; rather, I see them as a case of the evidence supporting the theory, and vice versa.

There are several questions that I have discussed previously, and which come to the fore now as we look at these passages of the *Iliad*. What does it mean to say that a line has been "interpolated"? We may have an idea of how and why it came to be in this specific location, but does that mean that it does not "belong" there now? How do the canons of textual criticism apply in these situations? For Bolling and others, the *external* evidence has nearly always seemed to be primary. But why should *internal* evidence be downplayed? And if the passage seems to read "better" without a given line and "worse" with it, should this, in the case of Homer, automatically mean that the line gets cut from the text? Don't performers perform "better" on some occasions than others, and while we may have a preference, is that the same as judging a reading to be "right" or "wrong"? For some these questions may have easy and decisive answers. But back to the text.

I follow Stephanie West's text for specific Ptolemaic papyri, except for those published subsequent to her 1967 book.

1.   *Iliad* III 302–312, as preserved in P40, with five "plus verses"; dated by S. West to between 285 and 250 BCE, but by M. West to the first half of the second century BCE.[76] Either way it is earlier than the 146/145 BCE date discussed in the previous chapter.

Immediate context: A duel has been agreed to between Menelaus and Paris. Agamemnon has just made a speech declaring the terms of the truce and duel, and has sacrificed lambs and poured wine on the ground. Interestingly, this is one of the few times when the death struggle of the sacrificial victims is described.[77] Soldiers on both sides are praying that anyone who breaks the conditions of the oaths may have their brains poured out on the ground and their wives controlled by (or sleep with) other men.

First, the "vulgate" text:

302   ὣς ἔφαν· οὐδ' ἄρα πώ σφιν ἐπεκράαινε Κρονίων.
        τοῖσι δὲ Δαρδανίδης Πρίαμος μετὰ μῦθον ἔειπεν·
        "κέκλυτέ μοι, Τρῶες καὶ ἐϋκνήμιδες Ἀχαιοί.
305   ἤτοι ἐγὼν εἶμι προτὶ Ἴλιον ἠνεμόεσσαν

---

[76]   S. West 1967:40; M. West 2001:90. Such redating of papyri does happen occasionally, based on a fresh look at and reanalysis of the script and other features. I follow S. West's edition, West 1967:40–58.
[77]   See Kitts 2005 for her interpretation of the implications of this.

ἂψ, ἐπεὶ οὔ πω τλήσομ' ἐν ὀφθαλμοῖσιν ὁρᾶσθαι
μαρνάμενον φίλον υἱὸν ἀρηϊφίλωι Μενελάωι.
Ζεὺς μέν που τό γε οἶδε καὶ ἀθάνατοι θεοὶ ἄλλοι,
ὁπποτέρωι θανάτοιο τέλος πεπρωμένον ἐστίν."
310 ἦ ῥα, καὶ ἐς δίφρον ἄρνας θέτο ἰσόθεος φώς,
ἂν δ' ἄρ' ἔβαιν' αὐτός, κατὰ δ' ἡνία τεῖνεν ὀπίσσω·
πὰρ δέ οἱ Ἀντήνωρ περικαλλέα βήσετο δίφρον.

302   Thus they spoke, but the son of Kronos would not yet
     grant them fulfillment.
  And Dardanian Priam spoke to them:
  "Hear me, Trojans and well-greaved Achaeans;
305   Indeed I am going to windy Ilion
  Again, since I will not dare to see with my own eyes
  My own son fighting with Menelaus dear to Ares;
  Zeus, no doubt, and the other immortal gods know
  To which of the two the fate of death has been
     destined."
310   He spoke, and then the godlike man placed the lambs
     onto his chariot,
  Then himself got on, and pulled the reins back;
  And Antenor got onto the well-made chariot beside
     him.

Next, the Ptolemaic papyrus P40:

302   [ὣς ἔφαν, εὐχό]μενοι, μέγα δ' ἔκτυπε μητίετα Ζεύς
302a   [. . . . .] φων ἐπὶ δὲ στεροπὴν ἐφέηκεν·
302b   [θησέμεναι γ]ὰρ ἔμελλεν ἔτ' ἄλγεά τε στοναχάς τε
302c   [Τρωσί τε καὶ] Δαναοῖ[σι] διὰ κρατερὰς ὑσ[μί]νας.
302d   [αὐτὰρ ἐπεί ῥ' ὅ]μοσέν τε τελεύτησέν [τε] τὸν ὅρκον,
303   [. . . . . . Δαρδανί]δ[η]ς Πρίαμος πρὸς μῦθον ἔειπ[ε·
304   ["κέκλυτέ μοι Τ]ρῶες καὶ Δάρδανοι ἠδ' [ἐ]πίκ[ουροι,
304a   [ὄφρ' εἴπω] τά μ[ε θυ]μὸς ἐνὶ στήθεσσιν ἀν[ώ]γε[ι.
305   [ἤτοι ἐ]γὼν εἶμι πρ[ο]τὶ Ἴλιον ἠνεμόεσσαν·
306   [ο]ὐ γάρ κεν τλαίην [ποτ' ἐν ὀφθα]λμοῖσιν ὁρᾶ[σθαι
307   [μα]ρνάμ[ε]νον φίλο[ν υἱὸν ἀρηϊφίλωι Μενελάωι·
308   [Ζεὺς μέν που] τό [γ]ε [οἶδε καὶ ἀθάνατοι θεοὶ ἄλλοι,
309   [ὁπποτέρωι θα]γάτοιο τέλ[ος πεπρωμένον ἐστίν."
310   [ἦ ῥα, καὶ ἐς δίφρο]ν ἄρ[νας θέτο ἰσόθεος φώς,

302   [Thus they spoke, pray]ing, and Zeus the counselor thun-
          dered greatly.
302a   [. . . . .] and let loose a bolt of lightening:
302b   [For he intended] to place further woes and groanings
302c   [Upon the Trojans and] Danaans through fierce battles.
302d   [But when he had] sworn and finished the oath,
303   [. . . . . . Dardan]ian Priam spoke this word:
304   ["Hear me, T]rojans and Dardanian allies;
304a   [While I say] what my heart in my breast is bidding me.
305   [Indeed] I am going to windy Ilion
          For I would not [ever] dare to see with my own eyes
          My own son fighting [with Menelaus dear to Ares;]
          [Zeus] and [the other immortal gods know]
          [To which of the two] the fate of dea[th has been destined."]
310   [He spoke, and then the godlike man placed] the la[mbs
          onto his chariot,]

The reconstruction of the beginning of line 302 ὣς ἔφαν εὐχόμενοι, 'thus they spoke, praying', occurs only in *Iliad* X 295 (although the singular participle occurs much more frequently): there Odysseus and Diomedes pray specifically to Athena, at some length, and she hears and in effect answers their prayers. Here the prayers are to Zeus, for any breaking of the oaths to be avenged. The "vulgate" has no mention of prayer, nor of Zeus thundering, just his reluctance to grant fulfillment to their wishes. In the papyrus, it appears that the poet continues with the idea of prayer; the verb κτυπέω is fairly rare, and generally seems to indicate trouble for one group, and maybe success for the other. But in *Iliad* XV 377, Zeus hears the prayer of Nestor, then ἔκτυπε 'crashed, thundered' to show he has heard his prayer; however he then gives help to the Trojans rather than the Greeks.

In the papyrus version, Zeus thunders and sends lightening (302a), but then (302b) 'was intending to place further woes and groanings upon [302c] both Trojans and Danaans. . .'; so no one is about to be helped. S. West points out that thunder after a prayer in Homer "is normally a sign that it will be fulfilled."[78] She also, along with other scholars, finds lines 302b and c acceptable, but 302d "extremely suspect," because in all of its many other occurrences it always follows the actual *swearing* of an oath.[79] However the *language* of oaths has been used already (269, 279, 280), twice by Agamemnon, so I don't see the line as quite

[78]   S. West 1967:53.
[79]   Ibid.

so objectionable. But this raises another question—if a line is used in an apparently "unique" way, does that prevent it from being "authentic"?

Line 302d has Priam as its subject; the Trojan preparation for the oaths has occurred in lines 245–258, so again it is not incongruous that Priam has finished his oath at this point. What is more interesting is the way in which the papyrus seems to emphasize Priam's fear of seeing his son Paris fight against Menelaus. In line 304 the papyrus has Priam talking only to Trojans and Trojan allies, as opposed to both Trojans and Greeks in the "vulgate." 304a adds a personal touch about Priam's internal unease, and in 306 the papyrus uses a potential optative rather than the future indicative, seeming to contribute to the emotional instability of Priam.

As in other passages to be considered, the papyrus gives the impression that it is a "version" of a performance with a somewhat heightened emotional tone. If this is so, what we have is apparently some sort of "transcript" of a particular performance.[80]

2.   *Iliad* III 338–339c, again as preserved in P40, with three "plus verses."

Immediate context: Lots have just been cast by Hector, and Paris' lot has "jumped out" first, indicating that he should have the first spear throw in his duel with Menelaus.[81] Paris now begins to arm himself. I start at line 330 in the Teubner, although P40 really only starts this section at line 338 (the previous line has three letters surviving, and apparently was quite different from our line 337[82]).

Teubner:

330   κνημῖδας μὲν πρῶτα περὶ κνήμῃσιν ἔθηκεν
       καλάς, ἀργυρέοισιν ἐπισφυρίοις ἀραρυίας·
       δεύτερον αὖ θώρηκα περὶ στήθεσσιν ἔδυνεν
       οἷο κασιγνήτοιο Λυκάονος, ἥρμοσε δ' αὐτῶι·
       ἀμφὶ δ' ἄρ' ὤμοισιν βάλετο ξίφος ἀργυρόηλον
335   χάλκεον· αὐτὰρ ἔπειτα σάκος μέγα τε στιβαρόν τε·
       κρατὶ δ' ἐπ' ἰφθίμωι κυνέην εὔτυκτον ἔθηκεν
       ἵππουριν· δεινὸν δὲ λόφος καθύπερθεν ἔνευεν·
       εἵλετο δ' ἄλκιμον ἔγχος, ὅ οἱ παλάμηφιν ἀρήρει.
       ὣς δ' αὔτως Μενέλαος ἀρήϊος ἔντε' ἔδυνεν.

---

[80] See Nagy passim for his use of this term; e.g. Nagy 2004:33–36.

[81] In general in the *Iliad* the warrior who strikes first is the one who comes off worse; e.g. Sarpedon versus Patroclus in book XVI. The fight between Achilles and Hector in book XXII is an exception, not least because it is the ultimate duel between two Homeric warriors.

[82] See S. West 1967:44, 54–55.

330   First he (i.e. Paris) put the greaves around his legs,
        fine ones, fitted with silver ankle-pieces.
        Second he put on his breastplate about his chest,
        of his brother Lycaon; and fitted it to himself.
        And about his shoulders he threw his silver-studded sword
335   of bronze, and then his shield great and sturdy.
        And upon his mighty head he put a well-made helmet
        with horse-hair crest; and terribly did the plume nod from
           above.
        And he took a stout spear, which fitted his hands.
        And likewise warlike Menelaus donned his battle gear.

P40:

338   εἴλε[το δ' ἄλκιμα] δοῦρε δύ[ω κεκορυθμένα χαλκῶι.
339   ὡς δ' αὔ[τως Μεν]έλαος ἀρήϊα [τεύχε' ἔδυνεν,
339a   ἀσπίδα κ[αὶ πήλη]κα φαεινὴ[ν καὶ δύο δοῦρε
339b   καὶ καλὰ[ς κνη]μῖδας ἐπισφ[υρίοις ἀραρυίας,
339c   ἀμφὶ δ' ἄ[ρ' ὤμοισι]ν βάλετο ξί[φος ἀργυρόηλον

338   And he took two [stout] spears, [tipped with bronze.
339   And like[wise Men]elaus donned his [warlike armor,
339a   His shield a[nd shin]ing helmet, [and two spears
339b   And fine greaves fitted [with ankle-pieces,
339c   And about his [shoulders] he threw his si[lver-studded
           sword.

Conceivably two different readers could come up with opposite conclusions
about this passage. One might say that the added lines are repetitive—we
have already had the arming of Paris, so lines dealing with that of Menelaus
are redundant. Conversely, another could want Menelaus to be given more
than just one line, as if Paris were stealing the limelight. Of course we are
fully expecting Paris to lose this duel, so giving him the longer arming scene
enhances the ominous nature of the passage.

   S. West discusses the papyrus variant lines in the light of "all the great
arming scenes in Homer."[83] She lists the following: *Iliad* V 735ff. (Athena), XI

---

[83] S. West, ibid. I notice that West omits the arming of Patroclus in *Iliad* XVI 130ff. Also all six
elements are not always present: in the passages from *Iliad* V and *Odyssey* xxii, the first three
items are missing.

16ff. (Agamemnon), XIX 364ff. (Achilles), and *Odyssey* xxii 122ff. (Odysseus); she further states that the order is always the same: 1) greaves, 2) cuirass (or breastplate), 3) sword, 4) shield, 5) helmet, and 6) spear (or spears). She makes the comment that it was particularly important to put on the shield before the helmet, for reasons of convenience: the plume of the helmet would interfere with the shield-strap if the helmet were donned before the shield.[84]

In considering the papyrus' "additional lines" 339abc, I observe firstly that the shield does still precede the helmet: indeed, items 4, 5, and 6 appear in order at the beginning, with greaves and sword being placed last. Now the preceding lines (328–338) have all dealt with the arming of Paris (using several lines repeated in other arming scenes), with that of Menelaus getting only the single line 339 in the "vulgate." The papyrus version gives Menelaus four lines instead of one, and moreover none of the three extra lines is repeated from the earlier description, indeed one is "unique" in Homer. Rather than Menelaus' arming being simply a repetition of that of Paris, it is more of a summary, with shield, helmet, and spears all mentioned in the same line. Thus one scholar's claim that the papyrus version "has brought down the Homeric passage to the level of primitive epic poetry" by unartistic and tedious repetition, which "only says that the armor of Menelaus was identical with that of Paris,"[85] is simply false, and overlooks the obvious: the second description relates to the first by *not* repeating it, which would perhaps be rather "tedious" (to use the same scholar's term), but rather by summarizing it, as mentioned above. In fact, the additional line 339a uses words for shield and helmet which are different from those used in Paris' arming. Thus the papyrus version still focuses upon Paris' arming, but also devotes some space to that of Menelaus: the two go together without any problems of "tedious" or "artless" repetition. (I note that, in contrast to van der Valk, Kirk suggests that a fuller description of Menelaus' arming would have underlined the unbalanced nature of the contest.[86] This seems to me as unlikely, if not more so, than van der Valk's suggestions.) In this connection I note other "abbreviated" scenes which mention lists of arms, such as *Iliad* XIII 264–265 (which is admittedly not an actual arming scene), where spears and shields appear in one line, helmets and breastplates in the other.[87]

Zenodotus, according to the scholia to Venetus A, had the lines in an order similar to those of P40, and Rengakos notes that Zenodotus' text has a striking parallel in the *Argonautica* of Apollonius of Rhodes, with the arming

---

[84] Ibid.
[85] van der Valk 1964:545–546.
[86] Kirk 1985:316.
[87] Cf. also Iliad XVIII 457ff. (Thetis requesting new armor for Achilles), and XIX 359ff.

of Aietes before his fight with Jason: the order of weapons corresponds identically, to the point that neither arming-scene includes mention of a sword.[88] This is a case in which the reading of Zenodotus can be shown to have a basis in an existing version of the text, rather than being a "subjective conjecture."

Thinking of the two versions from a performance perspective, one can imagine a singer on a particular occasion getting a heightened sense of the drama of the upcoming duel—it is clear after all that Paris is the weaker fighter; he has been allotted first strike, meaning he is going be the loser, so to speak; and so our particular singer gives Paris *two* spears, as well as making not Menelaus but his armor "warlike"; and then giving Menelaus four lines instead of one for his arming. These are variations that would seem perfectly natural as a way of performing this particular episode at a higher emotional level than on some other occasion.

Lines 339b and c occur elsewhere in Homer; line 339a does not, although its formulas πήληκα φαεινὴν and δύο δοῦρε occur elsewhere in Homer, the latter frequently in the same part of the line.[89] What does this prove? We know that the ancient Alexandrians seemed to have an aversion for repeated lines, an aversion shared by several modern scholars. In fact in the medieval manuscript Venetus A the "asterisk" sign was placed next to lines that Aristarchus noted occurred in other locations; if in addition the "obelos" sign was placed next to the asterisk, then in Aristarchus' judgment the line in question "belonged" in the other location, but not in the one in question.[90] This may have been understandable for the Alexandrians—but is it necessarily the right approach for us? Just because a line occurs elsewhere, even fairly closely to its current location, is this an indication that one of the occurrences must be "wrong"? *Iliad* VI 269 and 279 are identical and only ten lines apart, but as far as I know no edition omits one or other line.

3.   *Iliad* VI 280–292, as preserved in P480a,[91] with three "plus verses"; dated "Ptolemaic."

Immediate context: Hecuba has just tried to persuade her son Hector to rest, drink some wine, and pour a libation to Zeus and the other gods. Hector

---

[88]   Rengakos 1993:55–58.
[89]   For the "plus verses" 339abc, note:
          339a: cf. *Iliad* VI 322, XIII 527, *Odyssey* i 256, xii 228, xviii 228, xxii 101.
          339b: = *Iliad* XVIII 459; cf. III 331.
          339c: = *Iliad* II 45, etc.
          (Sutton 1997).
[90]   See Bird 2009 for a detailed and illustrated account of the critical signs in the Venetus A manuscript of the *Iliad*.
[91]   I follow the edition of Boyaval 1967:57–65.

declines, saying that the wine will weaken him, and that in his current state, covered with blood and gore, he is in no condition to offer libations to the gods. He gives her instructions in order to try and appease the wrath of Athena by taking her a richly woven robe.

Teubner:

"ἀλλὰ σὺ μὲν πρὸς νηὸν Ἀθηναίης ἀγελείης
280 ἔρχε', ἐγὼ δὲ Πάριν μετελεύσομαι, ὄφρα καλέσσω,
αἴ κ' ἐθέλησ' εἰπόντος ἀκουέμεν. ὥς κέ οἱ αὖθι
γαῖα χάνοι· μέγα γάρ μιν Ὀλύμπιος ἔτρεφε πῆμα
Τρωσί τε καὶ Πριάμωι μεγαλήτορι τοῖό τε παισίν.
εἰ κεῖνόν γε ἴδοιμι κατελθόντ' Ἄϊδος εἴσω,
285 φαίην κεν φίλον ἦτορ ὀϊζύος ἐκλελαθέσθαι."
ὣς ἔφαθ'· ἡ δὲ μολοῦσα ποτὶ μέγαρ' ἀμφιπόλοισιν
κέκλετο, ταὶ δ' ἄρ' ἀόλλισσαν κατὰ ἄστυ γεραιάς.
αὐτὴ δ' ἐς θάλαμον κατεβήσετο κηώεντα,
ἔνθ' ἔσάν οἱ πέπλοι παμποίκιλοι, ἔργα γυναικῶν
290 Σιδονιῶν, τὰς αὐτὸς Ἀλέξανδρος θεοειδὴς
ἤγαγε Σιδονίηθεν ἐπιπλοὺς εὐρέα πόντον
τὴν ὁδόν, ἣν Ἑλένην περ ἀνήγαγεν εὐπατέρειαν.

"But you, go to the shrine of Athena who carries the
        spoil,
280 and I will go and look for Paris, to call him,
    if perhaps he wishes to hear what I have to say. I wish for
        him the earth
    would gape right now; for the Olympian reared him as
    a great source of pain for the Trojans and for great-hearted
        Priam and his children.
    If I were to see him having gone down into Hades,
285 I would say that my own heart had forgotten its grief."
    Thus he spoke; and she went to the hall and called
    to her maids, and they gathered together the older women
        throughout the city.
    But she went down to the sweet-smelling chamber,
    Where her many-colored robes were, the work of Sidonian
290 Women, whom godlike Alexander himself
    Had led from Sidon when he sailed the wide sea,
    That journey on which he brought back Helen of the noble
        father.

Chapter 3

P480a:

280   "ἔρχευ, ἐγὼ] δὲ Πάριν μετελ[εύ]σομαι, ὄφρα καλέσσ[ω,

280a   ] <u>ον στονόεντα μ</u>[.....]ρ<u>ω</u>ᾳ . . α . τ . . ω . ο<u>υ</u>

    ]ι εἰπόντος ἀκουέμεν· ὥς κέ οἱ αὖθι

    γαῖα χάν]οι· μέγα γάρ μιν Ὀλύμπιος ἔτρ<u>α</u>φε πῆμα

    Τρωσί τε] καὶ Πριάμ<u>ῳ</u> μεγαλήτορι τοῖό τε παισίν·

    εἰ κεῖνόν] γε ἴδοιμι κατελθόντ' Ἄϊδος εἴσω,

285   φαίην κε] <u>φρέν' ἀτέρπου</u> ὀϊζύος ἐκλελαθέσθαι."

    <u>ὣς ἔφατ', ο]ὐδ' ἀπίθησ' Ἑκάβη, ταχὺ δ'</u> ἀ[μ]φιπόλοισι

    κέκλετο· ταὶ δ' ἄ]ρ' ἀόλλισσαν κατὰ ἄστ[υ] γεραιάς·

288   αὐτὴ δ' ἐς] θάλαμο<u>ν</u> κατεβήσετο κη<u>ω</u>έντα,

288a   <u>κέδρινον] ὑψερεφῆ ὅς γλήνη πολλ' ἐκεκεύθει</u>

288b   ] <u>φωριαμοῖσι παρί[στ]ατο δῖα γυνα[ικῶν</u>

    ἔνθ' ἔσάν οἱ]πέπλοι παμπο[ίκι]λοι ἔργα γυν[αικῶν

290   Σιδονίων, τὰς α]ὐτὸς Ἀλέξανδ[ρος θεοειδὴς

    ἤγαγε Σιδονίη]θεν, ἐπιπλ[ὼς εὐρέα πόντον,

    τὴν ὁδὸν ἣν Ἑλέ]νη[ν περ ἀνήγαγεν εὐπατέρειαν·

280   "You go, and I will go and look for Paris, to call him,

280a   <u>. . . . . carrier of woe? . . . . .</u>

    if perhaps he wishes] to hear what I have to say. I wish for
        him the earth

    would gape right] now; for the Olympian rear<u>ed</u> him as a
        great source of pain

    for the Trojans] and for great-hearted Priam and his chil-
        dren.

    If I were to see] him having gone down into Hades,

285   I would say] that my own <u>mind</u> had forgotten its <u>painful</u>
        grief."

    Thus he spoke,] <u>nor did Hecuba disobey, but quickly</u> called
    to her maids,] and they gathered together the older women
        throughout the city.

    But she went] down to the sweet-smelling chamber,

288a   <u>Made of cedar] which contained many noble</u>
        <u>treasures</u>

288b   <u>] queenly among women, she stood beside the</u>
        <u>chests</u>

    Where her] many-colored robes were, the work of Sidonian

290   Women, whom] godlike Alexand[er himself
Had led from Sidon] when he sail[ed the wide sea,
That journey on which he brought back He]le[n of the noble father.

Beginning this time with the first "plus verse," 282a, we see that it is poorly preserved, with the only complete word able to be made out being στονόεντα 'groaning, bringing or causing groans'. Elsewhere in Homer this word is used four times with βέλεα or βέλεμνα 'weapons' and once with κήδεα 'woes'. In this passage it conceivably could be referring to Paris, which would tie in with the following sentiment of Hector, that he wishes Paris might be swallowed up by the earth and go down to Hades. This would be not only a unique usage, but also a powerful way of comparing Paris to a spear that brings grief to others, in particular his own family members. And the usage fits in well here with the following words πῆμα 'bane, destruction', and ὀϊζύς 'sorrow, grief'. Similarly, line 285 in the papyrus has the uncommon adjective ἀτέρπου 'causing pain' used to describe Hector's sorrow; in contrast, the "vulgate" gives the adjective φίλον, which means little more here than 'my own' as referring to Hector's heart. The papyrus version is attributing to Hector a stronger sense of grief and sorrow than is our more familiar text. Once again we might imagine a performer feeling Hector's "pain" to an unusual degree, and using diction with a greater degree of emotional intensity.

In line 286, Hecuba, rather than just μολοῦσα 'going', rather *does not disobey,* and *quickly* calls her maidservants, intensifying the more mundane "vulgate" version. The formulaic phrase οὐδ' ἀπίθησ' occurs about twenty-five times in Homer, generally of Hera, Iris, Thetis, and Zeus, but also of humans such as Achilles and Agamemnon. The only other human female it is used of is Eurycleia in *Odyssey* xxii 492, after being ordered by Odysseus to assist with cleaning the hall after the deaths of the suitors. For a listener familiar with that story this has to add to the power of the phrase being used in this present context. One is also reminded of Telemachus and Penelope, but even then Penelope is not spoken of as 'not disobeying' her son.

In the two following lines, 287 and 288, we notice two seemingly minor textual variants (I pass over κηωίεντα for now): ἀόλλισσαγ κατὰ and θάλαμογ κατεβήσετο. These are clear examples of spelling reflecting pronunciation (in these two cases assimilation of a nasal to the following velar stop), in a way that presumably would not happen if the lines were being dictated slowly and carefully. Rather I suggest that these spellings convey the memory of a live performance, with all its speed and dramatic intensity.

Lines 288a and b are the remaining "plus verses." 288a recalls *Iliad* XXIV 192, where Priam is getting jewels and other precious materials in order to ransom the body of Hector, and telling Hecuba what he is planning to do. Priam also asks Hecuba what she thinks of his plan. The hearer of this slightly "longer" papyrus version will feel the poignancy of the connection between the two visits to the treasure chamber, the former by Hecuba at the command of Hector in order to appease the wrath of Athena, the second by Priam, to the dismay of Hecuba, in order to ransom the body of that same Hector.[92]

Line 288b and the following lines recall *Odyssey* xv 104, where Helen is taking the finest robe from her treasure chests as a gift for Telemachus. She too is called there δῖα γυναικῶν; and there is the added connection that Hecuba's robes came from the same journey that Paris was on when he brought back Helen to Troy. It is as if the poet, aware that he will soon be telling of the finest robe that Hecuba must give to Athena, the one that ἀστὴρ δ᾽ ὣς ἀπέλαμπεν 'shone like a star' and ἔκειτο δὲ νείατος ἄλλων 'lay underneath all the rest' (*Iliad* VI 295), makes a link to the robe of Helen with those same words (*Odyssey* xv 108), and hence Hecuba becomes like Helen for a brief moment. But what pains Helen brought to Hecuba! And those pains are being brought into the present context by means of the allusion to Priam in *Iliad* book XXIV.

To conclude: the poet has used more words and more intense words to express the grief of Hector; this has led to a more decisive reaction by Hecuba, which has then helped to make a connection with both Priam, Helen, Paris, and Hector himself. I repeat one of my earlier points: these "plus verses" are an inherent part of the story—of this particular version of the story, that in some ways has more emotional "power" than the version to which we are more accustomed. To write them off as "concordance interpolations"—lines merely inserted into a passage because of some connection from elsewhere—and hence needing to be "excised," means that we miss out on some significant intertextual relationships, and hence on some of the many linking references within the poem and between the *Iliad* and *Odyssey*.

4.　　*Iliad* XVII 566–584, as preserved in P501c, with four "plus verses"; dated "Ptolemaic."[93]

Immediate context: The Greeks are fighting over the body of Patroclus. Menelaus has just prayed to Athena to help protect him from Trojan weapons, and from Hector in particular.

---

[92] I note that the only other occurrence in Homer of ἐκεκεύθει is in the Cyclops' cave in *Odyssey* ix; there is also an occurrence of γλήνη there—meaning 'eyeball'.

[93] I follow Boyaval 1967:65–71 for the text of this papyrus.

Teubner:

"χαλκῶι δηϊόων· τῶι γὰρ Ζεὺς κῦδος ὀπάζει."
ὣς φάτο· γήθησεν δὲ θεὰ γλαυκῶπις Ἀθήνη,
ὅττί ῥα οἷ πάμπρωτα θεῶν ἠρήσατο πάντων.
ἐν δὲ βίην ὤμοισι καὶ ἐν γούνεσσιν ἔθηκεν,
570   καί οἱ μυίης θάρσος ἐνὶ στήθεσσιν ἐνῆκεν,
ἥ τε καὶ ἐργομένη μάλα περ χροὸς ἀνδρομέοιο
ἰχανάαι δακέειν· λαρόν τέ οἱ αἷμ' ἀνθρώπου·
τοίου μιν θάρσεος πλῆσε φρένας ἀμφὶ μελαίνας,
βῆ δ' ἐπὶ Πατρόκλωι, καὶ ἀκόντισε δουρὶ φαεινῶι.
575   ἔσκε δ' ἐνὶ Τρώεσσι Ποδῆς, υἱὸς Ἠετίωνος,
ἀφνειός τ' ἀγαθός τε, μάλιστα δέ μιν τίεν Ἕκτωρ
δήμου, ἐπεί οἱ ἑταῖρος ἔην φίλος εἰλαπιναστής·
τόν ῥα κατὰ ζωστῆρα βάλε ξανθὸς Μενέλαος
ἀΐξαντα φόβονδε, διάπρο δὲ χαλκὸν ἔλασσεν,
580   δούπησεν δὲ πεσών. ἀτὰρ Ἀτρεΐδης Μενέλαος
νεκρὸν ὕπεκ Τρώων ἔρυσεν μετὰ ἔθνος ἑταίρων.
Ἕκτορα δ' ἐγγύθεν ἱστάμενος ὤτρυνεν Ἀπόλλων,
Φαίνοπι Ἀσιάδηι ἐναλίγκιος, ὅς οἱ ἁπάντων
ξείνων φίλτατος ἔσκεν, Ἀβυδόθι οἰκία ναίων·

566   ". . . slaughtering with the bronze; for Zeus gives the glory
to him."
Thus he spoke, and the goddess bright-eyed Athena was
glad,
Because he had prayed to her first of all the gods.
And she (Athena) put strength into his (Menelaus') shoul-
ders and knees,
570   And into his breast she put the boldness of the fly,
Which even when driven away often from human skin
Is eager to bite, and pleasant to it is the blood of a man;
She filled him with such courage in his dark mind
And he stood over Patroclus and threw with his bright
spear.
575   And there was among the Trojans Podes, son of Eetion,
Wealthy and noble; and Hector honored him especially
Over the people, since he was his companion and friend at
the feast.

Yellow-haired Menelaus struck him on the belt
As he was rushing in fear, and he drove the bronze right
   through;
580   And he fell with a thud; but Menelaus son of Atreus
Dragged the corpse from amongst the Trojans into the
   group of his companions.
But Apollo stood near Hector and urged him on,
Appearing like Phaenops son of Asius, who was to him the
   most loved
Of all guests dwelling in his house at Abydus.

P501c:

566   "χαλκῶι δηϊόων· τῶι γὰρ Ζεὺς κῦδος ἔ[[ι]]δωκεν."
ὣ]ς φάτο, γήθησεν δὲ θεὰ γλαυκῶπις Ἀθήνη,
ὅ]ττί ῥά οἱ πάμπρωτα θεῶν ἠρήσατο πάντων·
ἐ]ν δὲ βίην ὤμοις καὶ ἐγ γούνασσιν ἔθηκεν,
570   κ]αί οἱ μυίης θάρσος ἐνὶ στήθεσσιν ἔθηκεν,
ἥ τε καὶ εἰργομένη περ μάλα χροὸς ἀνδρομέοιο
ἰσ]χανάαι δακέειν, λαρόν τέ οἱ αἷμ' ἀνθρώπου·
τωίου μιν θάρσους πλῆσεν φρένας ἀμφιμελαίνας,
574   βῆ] δ' ἐπὶ Πατρόκλωι μεγαλήτορι, τὸν δὲ κίχανεν
574a   κε]ίμενον, ἀμφὶ δέ μιμ βελέων ὀρυμαγδὸς ὀρώρει·
574b   στ]ῆ δὲ παρ' αὐτὸν ἰὼν καὶ ἀκόντισε δουρὶ φαεινῶι.
575   ἦ]ν δέ τις ἐν Τρώεσσι Ποδῆς, [π]αῖς Ἠετίωνος,
ἀ]φνηός τ' ἀγαθός τε· μάλιστα [δ]ὲ μήτιεν Ἕκτωρ
δ]ήμου, ἐπεί οἱ ἑταῖρος ἔην [φ]ίλο[ς] εἰλαπιναστής·
578   τ]όρ ῥα κατ' ἀσπίδα δουρὶ βάλεν ξανθὸς Μενέλαος·
578a   ἡ δ' οὐκ ἔγχος ἔρυτο, διὰ [π]ρὸ δὲ εἴσατο χαλκός,
578b   νειαίρηι δ' ἐγ γαστρὶ διὰ [ζωστ]ῆρος ἔλασσεν·

566   ". . . slaughtering with the bronze; for Zeus has given him
   glory."
567   Thus he spoke, and the goddess bright-eyed Athena was
   glad,
568   because he had prayed to her first of all the gods;
569   And she (Athena) put strength into his (Menelaus') shoul-
   ders and knees,
570   And into his breast she put the boldness of the fly,

Which even when[94] driven away often from human skin
Is eager to bite, and pleasant to it is the blood of a man;
She filled him with such courage in his dark mind

574   And he stood over great-hearted Patroclus, and reached him

574a   As he lay there, and around him the din of weapons arose;

574b   And he stood going by him, and he thrust with his shining spear.

575   And there was among the Trojans a certain Podes, son of Eetion,
Wealthy and noble; and Hector honored him especially
Over the people, since he was his companion and friend at the feast.

578   Him yellow-haired Menelaus struck with his spear on his shield;

578a   But it (the shield) did not stop the spear, but the bronze went right through

578b   And he drove it into his lower belly, through the belt.

This passage involves the Greeks fighting around the body of Patroclus, a frantic struggle that takes up a large part of book XVII of the *Iliad*. It is perhaps this franticness, as we have seen with other emotionally charged passages, that can help account for the "plus verses" and surrounding variation in the text in the papyrus version of this passage.

I note without comment the several small variations in lines 569–573; although in line 578 we see another example of assimilation, this time τόρ ῥα for τόν ῥα, reflecting the realities of oral performance rather than scribal dictation.

The charming fly simile is virtually the same in both versions; but when we get to the body of Patroclus, the papyrus has given Patroclus the epithet μεγαλήτορι 'great hearted', as well as the words τὸν δὲ κίχανεν//κείμενον 'and he reached him//as he lay there'. There seems to be some special care being shown towards Patroclus, although dead; there are four separate verbs relating to standing, reaching, going, as well as the comment that the 'din of weapons arose around him', to stress the fight going on for his body. Finally

---

[94] Some of the underlined text represents differences in the Greek text not reflected in the English.

we get the spear throw that has been "delayed" from the second half of line 574 to the second half of line 574b.

As with Patroclus, the papyrus version seems to emphasize the pathos of the death of Podes, although since the papyrus stops at line 578b we cannot be sure whether the word φόβονδε was in the next few lines. But the slightly more detailed description of the shield not stopping the spear, and of the spear going through Podes' lower belly, suggest a somewhat greater emotional involvement on the part of the poet.

Note: 17.578ab = 5.538–539, which refer to the killing of Deïcoön son of Pergasus, by Agamemnon. In each case the warrior killed is honored greatly, and his death evokes some amount of pity. I also note several cases of acoustical assimilation: ἐγ for ἐν in 569 and 578b; μιμ for μιν in 574a; τόρ for τόν in line 578. As suggested previously, these represent the way the language was heard rather than seen, and so hold clues as to performance aspects of the *Iliad* and *Odyssey*.

In this short examination of a handful of so-called "eccentric" Ptolemaic texts, we have seen that, far from being the result of careless scribal activity, what we are looking at can be viewed as functioning as a transcript of a live performance, and not only that, but a performance in which the "performer" could and did choose to heighten the emotional level by means of such things as variation in word choice, and intertextual links to other Homeric episodes; since a line of verse does not "operate" in isolation (or a vacuum), "importing" it into what may appear to be a "new" location has the effect of bringing with that line all of its thematic connections and connotations, which, in the "hands" of a skilled performer, can add power and emotion to an already dramatic performance. So our Ptolemaic papyri preserve much more than variant readings; they contain indications of the reality of live performances, of a performer's ability to "vary" his performance—in short, of multitextuality.

Appendix A

Other Instances of Multitextuality

I OFFER HERE some further illustrations of how the concept of "multitextuality" can be observed in other fields.

The first case comes from the New Testament, specifically the Book of Acts, whose text presents the textual critic with unusually thorny problems. Rather than there being one basic text with minor variants, there are two distinct forms of the text, called the Alexandrian and the Western. Both have early papyrus support, but the Western version is nearly 10 percent longer. One of the theories advanced to account for this state of affairs contends that a perceived freedom to "incorporate from oral tradition all kinds of additional details" led to a "wild and uncontrolled growth of the text during the first and second centuries."[1] In addition I notice with approval the rejection of the methodology by which one or more manuscripts are compared to an external standard, and the replacement of this methodology by one in which manuscripts are first compared directly with each other.[2] One might also think of how the existence of different versions of some episodes in the four Gospels can be thought of (at least in part) as surviving written records of one or more oral "performances."[3]

Secondly, I notice that in the history of the transmission of mathematical texts, particularly theorems, one finds significant variations which reflect traditions attributed to individuals. In the introduction (appropriately titled "Philologist, Heal thy Text") to his work on ancient and medieval geometrical texts, W. R. Knorr says: "Ironically, the office of personal succession can sometimes give rise to considerable freedom in the treatment of texts: the perceived essence is maintained, even as the verbal package is transformed."[4]

---

[1] Metzger 1971:259, 264.
[2] See above, p. 59; also Epp and Fee 1993:62.
[3] E.g. the two versions of the Lord's Prayer, in Matthew ch. 6 and Luke ch. 11. See p. 5 above.
[4] Knorr 1989:6.

Knorr proceeds to state that at least six different versions of the method of cube duplication presented by Hero of Alexandria (first century CE) survive, and he presents several of them in parallel columns.[5]

The remaining two examples come from the field of music, one early and the other modern. A paper written in 1974 by Leo Treitler argues that Gregorian plainchant melodies were composed and transmitted in a manner analogous to the composition and transmission of oral poetry.[6] Treitler identifies musical "formulas" as well as a "formulaic system," along essentially the same lines as the Parry-Lord formulation.

In addition I mention an unpublished Ph.D. dissertation which contains a detailed analysis of the improvised performances of the jazz pianist Bill Evans, with specific reference and comparison to Homeric oral formulaic techniques.[7] The jazz analogy is perhaps most pertinent when one bears in mind that no two performances are ever the same, and that none is more "correct" than another; the most that can be said is that one is more "inspired" (and inspiring) than another.[8]

---

[5] Ibid., chap. 1, pp. 11ff.

[6] Treitler 1974, whose title appropriately begins "Homer and Gregory . . . ."

[7] G. E. Smith 1983. I myself can recall being told, when learning to play jazz piano, to *transcribe* and *memorize* the improvised solos of the masters (from tape recordings), and then to use them as a basis for my own *original performances*. In future work I hope to explore further the relationship between Homeric oral poetry and jazz improvisation.

[8] I also draw attention to the following quote about jazz, with reference to a song entitled "Tiger Rag": "There was no single composer: The music was still part of an aural tradition" (quoted from Porter and Ullman 1993:5–6, 16, 31).

Appendix B

Glossary of Terms

I LIST HERE SOME ENGLISH AND LATIN TERMS which are frequently used in textual criticism.[1]
   The first three terms describe peculiarities which may occur within a passage of text; they are not themselves errors (although the terms are sometimes mistakenly used as if they were). The subsequent terms indicate types of error which may result from these first three, or from some other cause.

Term	Definition
homoeoteleuton	"same ending"—two words/sentences/lines/paragraphs of the text which end in the same letters. This appears to be the commonest of the three.
homoearcton	"same beginning"—two words/sentences/lines/paragraphs of the text which begin with the same letters.
homoeomeson	"same middle"—two words/sentences/lines/paragraphs of the text which have the same letters in the middle.
dittography	the writing twice of something that occurs once.
haplography	the writing once of something that occurs twice or more.
itacism, iotacism	an error resulting from the confusion of the letters and diphthongs η, ι, υ, ει, οι, υι, and η, the pronunciation of which converged to the same sound in Koine Greek.[2]

---

[1] See esp. Maas 1958, Metzger 1971, Pasquali 1952, Renehan 1969, Reynolds and Wilson 1991, Tarrant 1995, and West 1973.
[2] See Horrocks 1997:67–70 and 102–105.

lipography	an alternative name for haplography.
parablepsis	an occurrence in which the scribe's eye wanders from its proper place in the text; often facilitated by homoeoteleuton (or -arcton/-meson), and resulting in haplography.

These next terms, some Latin and some English, are used to describe aspects of the process of textual criticism. Several of these terms were mentioned in Chapters One and Two.

Term	*Definition*
recensio	a careful analysis of the available manuscript evidence, including establishing if possible the affiliations of mss.—i.e. stemmatics.
examinatio	the reconstruction of the text from the surviving manuscript evidence.
emendatio	the use of correction (and sometimes conjecture) when necessary to restore the original text.
divinatio	an older term for *emendatio*.
contaminatio	horizontal influence between mss.—when one ms. is used to "check" and alter another (conflation).
recentiores, non deteriores	"Later, not inferior"—later manuscripts may quite possibly contain old and hence good readings.
codex optimus	the best available manuscript, used by some editors virtually exclusively except when it is patently in error.
codices descripti	manuscripts which can be shown to be copies of another extant manuscript, and hence carry little or no independent weight.
eliminatio codicum descriptorum	The removal from consideration of *codices descripti*, i.e. the principle that manuscript evidence must be weighed, not counted.
lectiones singulares	readings which are unique to a particular manuscript, against the majority of other independent manuscripts.

eliminatio lectionum singularium   the removal of "singular" readings—i.e. when the majority of independent manuscripts are in agreement against one manuscript, the assumption that that manuscript's reading can be assumed to be incorrect.

utrum in alterum abiturum erat?   Which was liable to turn into the other? I.e. which variant can (best) explain the existence of the others?

lectio difficilior potior (or *melior*)   The harder reading is preferable (or better).

closed recension   variants only move "vertically," from exemplar to copy (Pasquali).

open recension   readings also move "horizontally," due to conflation.

internal evidence   a) the factors supporting a given reading such as style, grammar, orthography, logic (sometimes collectively labeled as "intrinsic" evidence, which relates to the author's most likely choice of words); b) the likelihood of this reading having arisen from another by scribal alteration, accidental or otherwise ("transcriptional" evidence, relating to what a scribe is most likely to have written).

external evidence   the number, age, and quality (including independence) of manuscripts in support of a reading.

autograph   the supposed document which the author himself wrote.

archetype   the (non-extant) document from which all our extant manuscripts are eventually derived.

hyparchetype   one or more non-extant documents deriving from the archetype, and from which a family of surviving manuscripts is derived.

Bibliography

BIFAO Bulletin de l'Institut français d'archeologie orientale de Caire.

MHV M. Parry, *The Making of Homeric Verse: The Collected Papers of Milman Parry*. Ed. Adam Parry. Oxford University Press, 1971.

OCD *Oxford Classical Dictionary*. 3rd ed. Oxford University Press, 1996.

OED *Oxford English Dictionary*, online. 3rd rev. ed. Oxford University Press.

Aland, K. and B. 1987. *The Text of the New Testament*. Leiden.

Allen, T. W. 1899. Review of Ludwich's *Homervulgata*. *Classical Review* 13:39–41.

——. 1924. *Homer: The Origins and the Transmission*. Oxford.

——, ed. 1931. *Iliad: Editio maior*. 3 vols. Oxford.

Apthorp, M. J. 1980. *The Manuscript Evidence for Interpolation in Homer*. Heidelberg.

——. 1999. "Homer's Winged Words and the Papyri: Some Questions of Authenticity." *Zeitschrift für Papyrologie und Epigraphik* 128:15–22.

Arend, W. 1933. *Die Typischen Szenen bei Homer*. Berlin.

Bengel, J. A. 1742. *Gnomon Novi Testamenti*. Tübingen.

Bird, G. D. 1994. "The Textual Criticism of an Oral Homer." In *Nile, Ilissos, and Tiber: Essays in Honour of Walter Kirkpatrick Lacey* (ed. V. J. Gray). *Prudentia* 26:35–52.

——. 2009. "Critical Signs—Drawing Attention to 'Special' Lines of Homer's *Iliad* in the Manuscript Venetus A." In Dué 2009:89–115.

Black, David Alan, ed. 2002. *Rethinking New Testament Textual Criticism*. Baker Academic.

Bolling, G. M. 1925. *The External Evidence for Interpolation in Homer*. Oxford.

——. 1944. *The Athetized Lines of the Iliad*. Baltimore.

——. 1950. *Ilias Atheniensium*. Lancaster, PA.

Boyaval, B. 1967. "Deux papyrus ptolemaïques." *BIFAO* 65:57–69.

Boyd, T. W. 1995. "Libri Confusi." *Classical Journal* 91.1:33–45.

Bibliography

Cherchi, P. 1995. "Italian Literature." In Greetham 1995:438–456.

Copland, A. 1980. *Music and Imagination.* Cambridge, MA.

Cross, F. M. 1992. "The Text behind the Text of the Hebrew Bible." In *Understanding the Dead Sea Scrolls* (ed. H. Shanks) 139–155. New York.

Davidson, O. M. 1988. "A Formulaic Analysis of Samples Taken from the *Shâhnâma* of Ferdowsi." *Oral Tradition* 3:88–105.

Denniston, J. D. and Page, D., eds. 1957. *Aeschylus' Agamemnon.* Oxford.

Dué, C. 2001. "Achilles' Golden Amphora in Aeschines' *Against Timarchus* and the Afterlife of Oral Tradition." *Classical Philology* 96:33–47.

——, ed. 2009. *Recapturing a Homeric Legacy: Images and Insights from the Venetus, a Manuscript of the Iliad.* Hellenic Studies 35. Washington, DC.

Edwards, M. W. 1992. "Homer and Oral Tradition: The Type-Scene." *Oral Tradition* 1992: 284–330.

Epp, E. J. 2002. "Issues in New Testament Textual Criticism: Moving from the Nineteenth Century to the Twenty-first Century." In Black 2002:17–76.

Epp, E. J. and Fee, G. D., eds. 1981. *New Testament Textual Criticism: Its Significance for Exegesis. Essays in Honour of Bruce M. Metzger.* Oxford.

——. 1993. *Studies in the Theory and Method of New Testament Textual Criticism.* Eerdmans.

Erbse, H., ed. 1969–1988. *Scholia Graeca in Homeri Iliadem I–VII.* Berlin.

Fenik, B. 1968. *Typical Battle Scenes in the Iliad.* Hermes Einzelschriften 21. Wiesbaden.

Finkelberg, M. 2000. "The Cypria, the Iliad, and the Problem of Multiformity in Oral and Written Tradition." *Classical Philology* 95:1–11.

Flinders Petrie, W. M. 1892. *Ten Years Digging in Egypt: 1881–1891.* London.

Garner, R. 1990. *From Homer to Tragedy: The Art of Allusion in Greek Poetry.* London.

Goold, G. P. 1988. *Ovid: Tristia.* Loeb Classical Library. Cambridge, MA.

Grant, John N., ed. 1989. *Editing Greek and Latin Texts.* New York.

Greek New Testament. 4th rev. ed. United Bible Societies. Stuttgart, 1993.

Greenlee, J. H. 1964. *Introduction to New Testament Textual Criticism.* Grand Rapids.

Greetham, D. C., ed. 1995. *Scholarly Editing: A Guide to Research.* Modern Language Association Guidelines. New York.

Grenfell, B. P. and Hunt, A. S. 1906. *The Hibeh Papyri.* London.

Hainsworth, J. B. 1970. "The Criticism of an Oral Homer." *Journal of Hellenic Studies* 90: 90–98.

Haslam, M. 1997. "Homeric Papyri and Transmission of the Text." In Morris and Powell 1997:55–100.

Heubeck, A., West, S., and Hainsworth, J. B. 1988. *A Commentary on Homer's Odyssey*, vol. I: *Books I-VIII*. Oxford.

Horrocks, G. 1997. *Greek: A History of the Language and Its Speakers*. London.

Housman, A. E., ed. 1903. *M. Manilii: Astronomicon, Liber Primus*. London.

Janko, R. 1982. *Homer, Hesiod, and the Hymns: Diachronic Development in Epic Diction*. Cambridge.

——. 1992. *The Iliad: A Commentary*, vol. IV: *Books 13-16*. Cambridge.

Jensen, M. Skafte. 1980. *The Homeric Question and the Oral-Formulaic Theory*. Copenhagen.

Kilpatrick, G. D. 1981. "Conjectural Emendation in the New Testament." In Epp and Fee 1981:349–360.

Kirk, G. S. 1962. *The Songs of Homer*. Cambridge.

——, ed. 1985. *The Iliad: A Commentary*, vol. I: *Books 1-4*. Cambridge.

——, ed. 1990. *The Iliad: A Commentary*, vol. II: *Books 5-8*. Cambridge.

Kitts, M. 2005. *Sanctified Violence in Homeric Society: Oath-Making Rituals and Narratives in the Iliad*. Cambridge.

Knorr, W. B. 1989. *Textual Studies in Ancient and Medieval Geometry*. Birkhaüser.

Koester, H. 1987. *Introduction to the New Testament*, vol. 2: *History and Literature of Early Christianity*. New York.

Labarbe, J. 1949. *L'Homère de Platon*. Liège.

Lang, M. L. 1983. "Reverberation and Mythology in the *Iliad*." In *Approaches to Homer* (ed. C. A. Rubino and C. W. Shelmerdine) 140–164. Austin.

Lascaris, J. 1517. *Σχόλια παλαιὰ τῶν πάνυ δοκίμων εἰς τὴν Ὁμήρου Ἰλιάδα*. Rome.

Leaf, W., ed. 1902. *The Iliad*. London.

Lord, A. B. 1960. *The Singer of Tales*. Cambridge, MA.

——. 1991. *Epic Singers and Oral Tradition*. Ithaca.

——. 1994. *The Singer Resumes the Tale*. Ed. M. L. Lord. Ithaca.

Ludwich, A. 1898. *Die Homervulgata als voralexandrinisch erwiesen*. Leipzig.

Luzio, A. di. 1969. "I papiri omerici d'epoca tolemaica e la costituzione del testo dell'epica arcaica." *Rivista di Cultura Classica e Medioevale* 11:3–152.

Maas, P. 1958. *Textual Criticism*. Trans. B. Flower. Oxford.

Maehler, H. 1996. "Greek Papyrology." OCD, 1109–1111.

Magoun, F. P., Jr., trans. 1963. *The Kalevala*. Compiled by Elias Lönnrot. Cambridge, MA.

Mahaffy, J. P. 1891. *The Flinders Petrie Papyri*. Dublin.

Bibliography

Mazon, P. 1943. *Introduction à l'Iliade*. With the collaboration of P. Chantraine, P. Collart, and R. Langumier. Paris.

McGann, J. J. 1992. *A Critique of Modern Textual Criticism*. Charlottesville, VA.

Metzger, B. M. 1971. *A Textual Commentary on the Greek New Testament*. New York.

———. 1992. *The Text of the New Testament: Its Transmission, Corruption, and Restoration*. 3rd ed. Oxford.

Monro, D. B., and Allen, T. W., eds. 1920. *Homeri Opera (Iliad)*. 3rd ed. Oxford.

Morris, I., and Powell, B., eds. 1997. *A New Companion to Homer*. Leiden.

Muellner, L. 1976. *The Meaning of Homeric EYXOMAI through Its Formulas*. Innsbrucker Beiträge zur Sprachwissenschaft 13. Innsbruck.

Nagy, G. 1970. *Greek Dialects and the Transformation of an Indo-European Process*. Cambridge, MA.

———. 1990. *Greek Mythology and Poetics*. Ithaca. Rev. 1992.

———. 1996a. *Poetry as Performance: Homer and Beyond*. Cambridge.

———. 1996b. *Homeric Questions*. Austin.

———. 1997. "Homeric Scholia." In Morris and Powell 1997:101–122.

———. 2003. *Homeric Responses*. Austin.

———. 2004. *Homer's Text and Language*. Champaign.

———. 2009. "Traces of an Ancient System of Reading Homeric Verse in the Venetus A." In Dué 2009:133–157.

Naveh, J. 1992. "Semitic Epigraphy and the Antiquity of the Greek Alphabet." *Kadmos* 31:143–152.

Nickau, K. 1977. *Untersuchungen zur textkritischen Methode des Zenodotos von Ephesos*. Berlin.

Nisbet, R. G. M. 1991. "How Textual Conjectures Are Made." *Materiali e discussioni per l'analisi dei testi classici* 26:65–91.

Parry, M. 1971. *The Making of Homeric Verse: The Collected Papers of Milman Parry*. Ed. Adam Parry. Oxford [abbreviated as *MHV*].

Pasquali, G. 1952. *Storia della tradizione e critica del testo*. 2nd ed. Florence.

Pfeiffer, R. 1968. *History of Classical Scholarship: From the Beginnings to the End of the Hellenistic Age*. Oxford.

———. 1976. *History of Classical Scholarship, from 1300 to 1850*. Oxford.

Pickens, R. T., ed. 1978. *The Songs of Jaufré Rudel*. Toronto.

Porter, L., and Ullman, M. 1993. *Jazz: From Its Origins to the Present*. Prentice Hall.

Powell, B. 1991. *Homer and the Origin of the Greek Alphabet*. Cambridge.

——. 1997. "Homer and Writing." In Morris and Powell 1997:3–32.

Reeve, Michael D. 1989. "Eliminatio codicum descriptorum: A Methodological Problem." In Grant 1989:1–35.

Reiman, D. H. 1995. "Nineteenth-Century British Poetry and Prose." In Greetham 1995:308–330.

Renehan, R. 1969. *Greek Textual Criticism: A Reader.* Cambridge, MA.

Rengakos, A. 1993. *Der Homertext und die hellenistischen Dichter. Hermes* Einzelschriften 64. Stuttgart.

Reynolds, L. D., ed. 1983. *Texts and Transmission: A Survey of the Latin Classics.* Oxford.

Reynolds, L. D. and Wilson, N. G. 1991. *Scribes and Scholars: A Guide to the Transmission of Greek and Latin Literature.* 3rd ed. Oxford.

Rhodes, E. F. 1981. "Conjectural Emendations in Modern Translations." In Epp and Fee 1981:361–374.

Robinson, Maurice A. 2002. "The Case for Byzantine Priority." In Black 2002:125–140.

Septuaginta. 2 vols. Ed. A. Rahlfs. Stuttgart, 1935.

Shipp, G. P. 1972. *Studies in the Language of Homer.* Cambridge.

Smith, G. E. 1983. *Homer, Gregory, and Bill Evans? The Theory of Formulaic Composition in the Context of Jazz Piano Improvisation.* Ph.D diss., Harvard University.

Smith, M. F. 1992. *Lucretius: De Rerum Natura.* Loeb Classical Library. Cambridge, MA.

Snodgrass, A. 1998. *Homer and the Artists: Text and Picture in Early Greek Art.* Cambridge.

Speer, M. B. 1995. "Old French Literature." In Greetham 1995:382–416.

Strugnell, J. 1974. "A Plea for Conjectural Emendation in the New Testament." *Catholic Biblical Quarterly* 36:543–558.

Sutton, D. F. 1997. *Homer in the Papyri: A Computerized Database.* Irvine, CA.

Tanselle, G. T. 1992. *A Rationale of Textual Criticism.* Philadelphia.

——. 1995. "The Varieties of Scholarly Editing." In Greetham 1995:9–32.

Taplin, O. 1986. "Homer." In *The Oxford History of the Classical World* (eds. J. Boardman, J. Griffin, and O. Murray) 50–77. Oxford.

Tarrant, R. J. 1989. "The Reader as Author: Collaborative Interpolation in Latin Poetry." In Grant 1989:121–162.

——. 1995. "Classical Latin Literature." In Greetham 1995:93–148.

Thiel, H. van, ed. 1991. *Homeri Odyssea.* Hildesheim.

——, ed. 1996. *Homeri Ilias.* Hildesheim.

Tov, E. 1992. *Textual Criticism of the Hebrew Bible*. Minneapolis.

Treitler, L. 1974. "Homer and Gregory: The Transmission of Epic Poetry and Plain-chant." *Music Quarterly* 60:333–372.

Turner, E. G. 1968. *Greek Papyri: An Introduction*. Oxford.

van der Valk, M. H. A. L. H. 1949. *Textual Criticism of the Odyssey*. Leiden.

——. 1963/1964. *Researches on the Text and Scholia of the Iliad* I/II. Leiden.

von der Muehll, P. 1962. *Homeri Odyssea*. Stuttgart.

Watkins, C. 1995. *How to Kill a Dragon: Aspects of Indo-European Poetics*. Oxford.

West, M. L. 1973. *Textual Criticism and Editorial Technique*. Stuttgart.

——. 1990. "Archaische Heldendichtung: Singen und Schreiben." In *Der Übergang von der Mündlichkeit zur Literatur bei den Griechen* (ed. W. Kullmann and M. Reichl) 33–50. Tübingen.

——, ed. 1998. *Homeri Ilias* I (Teubner). Stuttgart.

——, ed. 2000. *Homeri Ilias* II (Teubner). Munich.

——. 2001. *Studies in the Text and Transmission of the Iliad*. Munich.

West, S., ed. 1967. *The Ptolemaic Papyri of Homer*. Papyrologica Coloniensia 3. Cologne.

——. 1988. "The Transmission of the Text." In Heubeck, West, and Hainsworth 1988: 33–48.

Westcott, B. F. and Hort, F. J. A. 1882. *Introduction to the New Testament in the Original Greek*. New York. Reprint Hendrickson, 1988.

Wolf, F. A. 1985 [1795]. *Prolegomena ad Homerum*. Halle, 1795. Trans., with introduction and notes, A. Grafton, G. W. Most, and J. E. G. Zetzel. Princeton, 1985.

Zuntz, G. 1946. *The Text of the Epistles: A Disquisition upon the Corpus Paulinum*. Schweich Lectures. London.

Index Locorum

General Index

accentual variants, 56

additional lines. *See* plus verses

Aeschines, 30, 44, 61, 71, 72; *Against Timarchus*, 71

Aland, K., 2n4, 13, 65n23

Alexandrians, 26, 31, 32, 38, 40n61, 49, 56, 70, 74, 75, 85, 92

Allen, T. W., 2n3, 16n62, 31n21, 46, 50, 57, 58, 62, 64n15, 65, 70, 71, 75, 78

Apollonius Rhodius, 27, 37, 38, 45; *Argonautica*, 51, 91

Apthorp, M. J., 48–56

archetype, 12–19, 24, 25, 28, 40–47, 53–56

Arend, W., 53n122

Aristarchus of Samothrace, 26, 30n15, 31, 32n25, 36, 53, 54, 55, 56, 57, 66, 74, 78, 80n.o, 81, 92

Aristonicus, 38, 39, 49n110

Aristophanes (comic playwright), 18, 45

Aristophanes of Byzantium, 26

arming scenes, 90–92

Athenaeus, 35, 37

athetesis, 34, 38, 53, 80

autograph, 1, 13, 24

Bengel, J. A., 3, 4

Bentley, Richard, 4, 12, 21, 22

best text. See *codex optimus*

Bird, G. D., 27n1, 53n127, 92n90

Boiardo, Matteo Maria, 44

Bolling, G. M., 31n23, 32n25, 38, 41n62, 42, 48–56, 85, 86

Boyd, T. W., 42n67

Byzantine period, 16n63, 18, 30, 63, 64, 66

cacoethes coniciendi, 25n108

Cherchi, P., 44n76

Cicero, 7, 42n67

codex optimus, 10, 11

codices descripti, 3, also see Appendix B

collation, 2, 14, 15, 32, 65

compression (contraction), 48, 49, 55

conjecture, 2, 9, 12, 19–26, 25, 31, 50, 51, 56, 85; "subjective conjecture", 26, 31n22, 36, 92

contaminatio (contamination, conflation), 3n10, 14, 15, 16, 17, 28, 32, also see Appendix B

115